TEC

**FRIENDS
OF ACP**

3 1833 04750 900

D0069701

The Dharma of Dragons and Daemons

THE Dharma OF Dragons AND Daemons

Buddhist Themes in Modern Fantasy

David R. Loy
and Linda Goodhew

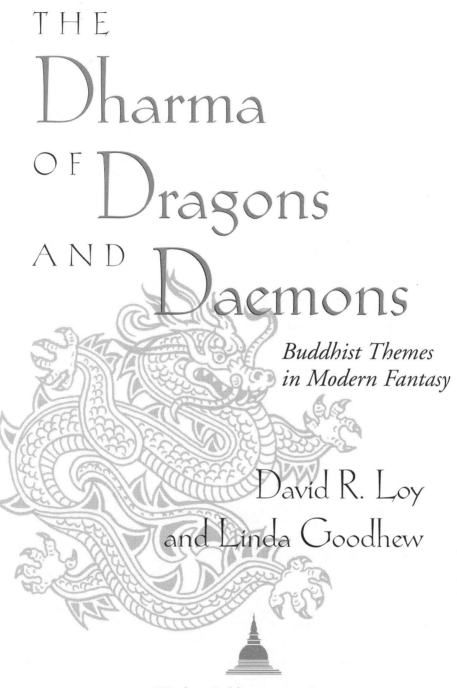

Wisdom Publications • Boston

Wisdom Publications
199 Elm Street
Somerville, MA 02144 USA
www.wisdompubs.org

© 2004 David R. Loy and Linda Goodhew
All rights reserved.

First Edition
09 08 07 06 05 04
6   5   4   3   2   1

No part of this book may be reproduced in any form or by any means, electronic or
mechanical, including photography, recording, or by any information storage or retrieval
system or technologies now known or later developed, without permission in writing
from the publisher.

Library of Congress Cataloging-in-Publication Data
Loy, David, R. 1947–
  The dharma of dragons and daemons : Buddhist themes in modern fantasy / David
Loy and Linda Goodhew.—1st ed.
    p. cm.
  Includes bibliographical references and index.
  ISBN 0-86171-476-8 (pbk. : alk. paper)
  1. Fantasy fiction--History and criticism. 2. Buddhism and literature. 3. Buddhism
in literature. 4. Tolkien, J. R. R. (John Ronald Reuel), 1892–1973. Lord of the rings.
5. Miyazaki, Hayao, 1941– Criticism and interpretation. 6. Pullman, Philip, 1946–
His dark materials. 7. Le Guin, Ursula K., 1929– Earthsea. 8. Ende, Michael. Momo.
I. Goodhew, Linda. II. Title.
  PN3435.L68 2004
  809.3'8766609382943—dc22
                                        2004015423

Earlier versions of most of these chapters have been published in various places. Permission
from the following journals and publishers to reprint is gratefully acknowledged.

"*The Dharma of the Rings*: A Myth for Engaged Buddhism?" in *Kyoto Journal* 56 (Winter
2004).

"*Momo*, Dogen and the Commodification of Time" in *Journal of the Faculty of
International Studies*, Bunkyo University (Shonan), 2001. Revised version reprinted in
Kronoscope: Journal for the Study of Time, new series, vol. 2:1, Leiden: Brill, 2002.

"The Dharma of Miyazaki Hayao: Revenge vs. Compassion in *Nausicaa* and *Mononoke*"
in *Journal of the Faculty of International Studies*, Bunkyo University (Shonan), 2004.

"Violence and Nonviolence in the *Anime* of Miyazaki" in *Nihon Jidoubungaku*, ed.
Nihon Jidoubungakusha Jokai (Tokyo: Bunkei), July/August 2004.

Wisdom Publications' books are printed on acid-free paper and meet the guidelines for
permanence and durability set by the Council of Library Resources.

Cover design by Patrick O'Brien
Interior design by Jeff Potter

Printed in Canada

To our fantastic mothers
Irene Loy and Margaret Goodhew
and their grandson
Mark Loy Goodhew
who loves fantasy

Contents

Foreword

A TRUE REALIZATION will be true in all times and cultures, available to be found by anyone. This book, exploring the appearance of Buddhist wisdoms in unexpected places, and with its profound recognition of the importance of story and myth to our ways of moving through the world, is a provocative confirmation of the teaching found in one of the most central of Buddhist texts. The Lotus Sutra tells us that the rain that falls on multitudinous landscapes and is taken in by many different animals and plants remains one rain; that the sea's flavor is salt, whatever coastline it touches. For its illustration of that alone, the contribution David Loy and Linda Goodhew offer here is significant.

But the real value of these pages lies in the way *The Dharma of Dragons and Daemons* investigates the deep questions of our current times—questions not different from those that faced Shakyamuni Buddha 2,500 years ago. How are we to live once we have entered into an aware engagement with suffering? What is the right action of compassion in the face of greed, delusion, and hate? That the Buddha's discoveries can be useful in seeing our way two and a half millennia later is not surprising. What exhilarates in this book is the way that making conscious the intersection of those discoveries with the imaginations of Tolkien, Le Guin, Ende, Miyazaki, and Pullman deepens our understanding not only of the fantasy tales and films considered here, but also of the Dharma itself.

This is a book whose pleasures reverberate profoundly, and a book that holds in its words the energies of genuine awakening. Its effects go deeper than the intellect, they penetrate to the heart. Let us praise the originality of David Loy and Linda Goodhew's thinking, the clarity of their writing, the pleasure of their sentences, and the important contribution they make to the ongoing dialogue of Buddhism and Western culture. Nine bows to them for bringing forth this superb book.

—JANE HIRSHFIELD

Acknowledgments

WE ARE BOTH VERY GRATEFUL to Josh Bartok
at Wisdom Publications and copy editor John LeRoy, whose
many suggestions have improved almost every page of this book.
Had we not resisted some of their editorial advice, it probably would
have been better still. We also wish to thank Mihoko Tanaka,
Stephanie Kaza, and Mihoko Nomura for their help in various ways.
Needless to say, whatever defects remain are our responsibility.

1

Fantastic Dharma

*Fantasy is true, of course. It isn't factual, but it is true.
Children know that. Adults know it too, and that is precisely why many of them are afraid of fantasy. They know
that its truth challenges, even threatens, all that is phony,
unnecessary, and trivial in the life they have let themselves
be forced into living.*

—Ursula K. Le Guin

I N   O R D E R   T O   L I V E , we need air, water, food,
shelter...and stories. One of the ways language makes us human
is by enabling us to create and share stories about what the world
is, who we are, and what we are to do while we are here. Our
minds seek their sustenance as much as our bodies seek food.
Consciously or unconsciously, stories order a complicated, often confusing world and give us models of how to live in it. They include
creation myths, folk and fairy tales, legends about gods and heroes,
Homeric epics and Norse sagas, Greek tragedy and Japanese Noh
dramas, histories of kings and kingdoms, novels and radio plays,
movies and television soap operas, some video and Internet games, and
fantasies of strange people in strange worlds "long ago and far away."

Until a few millennia ago, almost all stories were oral, and even a few centuries ago they were more often heard than read. Widespread literacy created new possibilities: the novel, most notably, along with shorter variants available in other forms such as magazines, newspapers, and comic books. Radio, then movies, television, and now the Internet have inundated us with new stories, largely because they have become commodities to be bought and sold (or dangled as bait by advertisers). With stories too, mass production and consumption encourage the lowest common denominator. Just as fast-food franchises beckon us with their high-sugar, high-fat snacks, so do video cassettes and DVDs of highly sexed and violent films lure us whenever boredom threatens the attention of an increasingly jaded audience.

The best stories, however, are more than entertainment. Traditionally the most important ones have been religious. According to the philosopher Arthur Schopenhauer, religion is the metaphysics of the masses, but it is just as true to label philosophy the religion of intellectuals. Theologians like to argue about doctrines, and religious institutions elevate those claims into dogmas, but for most of us it is chiefly the *stories* that we find meaningful, because stories speak to us and move us in ways that concepts do not. The birth of Jesus in a manger, because there was no room in the inn; the Last Supper, followed by the betrayal of Judas and Christ's agony on the cross; his resurrection, victorious over death—these narratives are what most Christians relate to, not the niceties of the Nicene Creed. Until recently, at least, Bible tales from the Old and New Testaments served as the "core stories" of Western civilization. Allusions to

them were embedded everywhere: Renaissance sculpture and painting, Bach's cantatas and Handel's oratorios, the epic poetry of Milton
and Blake. The success of Mel Gibson's "The Passion of the Christ"
reminds us that these stories have not lost their attraction.

Buddhism, too, can be seen as a collection of stories. The life of
Shakyamuni Buddha forms the core, especially such crucial incidents as his leaving home and his great awakening under the Bodhi
tree. According to legend, his father surrounded young Gotama
with healthy youthful people, so it was utterly shocking when he
eventually encountered a sick person, an old person, a corpse, and
finally a world-renouncer—which led him to renounce his own royal
position and become a forest ascetic. The power of this story is not
affected by the fact that it does not seem to be literally true.[1] Historical
or not, it remains a deeply moving myth, dramatically reminding
us not to repress awareness of illness, aging, and mortality, but to
allow that awareness to motivate a spiritual quest for the meaning
of our life and our death.

What was the great awakening that crowned this quest? What did
the Buddha realize that led to his liberation? The necessary ambigu-
ity of his enlightenment, for us, makes his realization less a doctrine
than a myth—the central myth—of Buddhism. To be a Buddhist is
to be gripped and motivated by this myth, to attempt to live up to
the Buddha's quest as one's own core story.

Myths do not gain their meaning because the incidents they describe actually occurred. If they are "true," it is because they evoke
something essential about who we are. J.R.R. Tolkien believed that
what he wrote in *The Lord of the Rings* was true, because "legends

and myths are largely made of 'truth,' and indeed present aspects of it that can only be received in this mode; and long ago certain truths and modes of this kind were discovered and must always reappear."[2] The theologian Paul Tillich distinguished "unbroken myth" (understood to be literally true) from "broken myth" (no longer believed to be historically true, but still held to have deep significance). In place of broken myth, however, the Anglican bishop Richard Holloway has suggested that we think in terms of *breaking open a myth*. The meaning of a myth is something contained within it, and often obscured by the details of the story, so if we want to taste its fruit we need to break through its skin. To reach the living heart-wood we must penetrate the hardened bark.

We need such myths to live by, as the mythologist Joseph Campbell put it. They are not crutches for those who cannot take too much reality, for we need them to figure out what is real and important about the world and our being in it. From a spiritual per-spective, then, the point is not to get rid of our myths but to become more aware of what they are. Myths change us: when we live a myth, that myth is also living us. One of the most pernicious myths is the myth of a life without myth. A few people become spiritually ill because they lose their myth and do not know how to find an-other one, but for most people the myth of no myth means they have been captured by the dominant myths of their culture—myths so prevalent that they are unaware of them, like the fish that does not notice the water it swims in.

The Pali canon—the earliest record we have of the teachings of the historical Buddha—is full of stories. The Buddha taught for forty-five years, and many incidents in his long career are preserved in its "three baskets" (*Tipitaka*). The third basket, the Abhidharma, attempts to summarize his doctrine into a more succinct and abstract philosophy, but the Sutras and the Vinaya—the other two baskets—always present the context for each of his talks: where it occurred and who was there. "Thus have I heard..." If those stories are often no more than the occasion for a teaching, each teaching is nevertheless placed within a larger narrative involving people who gather together to hear what the Buddha has to say. When we study the earliest records of the Buddhadharma, we read stories.

Buddhism has many other stories, of course. The non-canonical Jataka tales teach moral virtues by recounting the previous lifetimes of Shakyamuni, when he was developing his wisdom and selfless compassion as an animal *bodhisattva* (a "Buddha-in-training"). Later scriptures such as the Lotus Sutra and the Avatamsaka Sutra are basically long narratives that present their teachings by embedding stories within stories, often in the form of parables. Few Tibetans could explain anything about the basic Madhyamika-Yogachara philosophy of Tibetan Buddhism, yet most of them are familiar with stories about its founding fathers: tales from the lives of Padmasambhava, Marpa, Milarepa, and many others. The same is true for Japanese and Chinese people with regard to Chan/Zen Buddhism. Many who have never done any Zen meditation are familiar with its foundational legends about Bodhidharma and the sixth patriarch.

How many of these stories are literally true? Historical scholarship raises questions about most of them, yet the basic issue, for

Buddhists at least, is whether a myth inspires and empowers us to follow the Middle Path in a fruitful way. The problem with myth is not historical veracity but the tendency for stories, like more conceptual teachings, to fossilize and lose their ability to speak meaningfully. That is all the more likely to happen, of course, when teachings and stories are translated into very different cultures. Buddhism changed radically when it spread to China and Tibet, but at least both of those host societies were also premodern. The challenge involved in adapting what was originally an Iron Age religion to our postmodern high-tech world is of a different order of magnitude. In many cases, teachings need to be revivified by finding new vocabularies to express their core truths, perhaps even new methodologies to help realize those truths.

In the case of Buddhist myth, however, we wonder if new stories are needed that relate more directly to the experience of (post)modern people living in the twenty-first century. Where do we find those myths today?

This book is about such Buddhist stories: not about stories to be found in Buddhism, but about the "Buddhism" to be found in some modern stories. More precisely, it is about the Dharma—the basic teachings of Buddhism—as presented in some of the classics of contemporary fantasy: in J. R. R. Tolkien's *The Lord of the Rings,* in Michael Ende's children's novel *Momo,* in some animated films by Japan's *anime* master Hayao Miyazaki, in Philip Pullman's trilogy *His Dark Materials,* and in Ursula K. Le Guin's *Earthsea* series. With one insignificant exception (in the conclusion to Pullman's fantasy), none of these makes any reference to Buddhism, but that is hardly a shortcoming. On the contrary, it makes their Buddhist resonances all the more interesting and important, given our concern to re-present the Dharma in modern forms—in "Buddhist" myths that speak to our present condition, depicting it symbolically and emotionally as well as intellectually.

The need for such stories is not new. Buddhism, first introduced to Europe in the late eighteenth century by William Jones, Friedrich Schlegel, and other scholars, quickly began to influence philosophers such as Hegel, Schopenhauer, and Nietzsche. Naturally these thinkers emphasized its doctrinal implications, for theory was what they and other European intellectuals were interested in. Europe was in the midst of its own religious crisis—soon to be aggravated by Darwinism—and it was Buddhism's more rational attributes that were so attractive to those seeking to separate its metaphysical and ethical core from the magical and superstitious elements. Later Asian proselytizers such as Dhammapala and Soen Shaku were also eager to stress the scientific nature of Buddhism, while D.T. Suzuki focused on aspects of Zen that were consistent with contemporaneous Western thinking in psychology and philosophy.

Despite the debt that Western Buddhists owe to many of these figures, something was lost in that initial translation, or left behind: the role of stories, which for most Asian Buddhists continues to be the aspect that speaks most directly to them. Of course, we now have the Jataka tales and the songs of Milarepa, the Lotus Sutra and the Sixth Patriarch Sutra, which have become widely available in Western languages. Yet they remain *Asian* stories, which Westerners inevitably view through a cultural filter. Coming as they do from very different places, times, and cultures, they fascinate us—but their exoticism also distances us. That such myths are foreign to our civilization is both their attraction and their limitation. Perhaps the real challenge, for a westernizing Buddhism, is not only to express traditional Buddhist teachings in modern categories, but to find or create Dharma stories that resonate deeply with our contemporary Western spiritual inclinations. This book discusses some outstanding recent examples.

❧

The Lord of the Rings may not seem very susceptible to a Buddhist reading, given its uncompromising dualism between good and evil and its evident endorsement of violence against those who are evil (our topic in Chapter 4). Nevertheless, Chapter 2, "The Dharma of Engagement," presents Tolkien's story as a spiritual quest readily understandable in Buddhist terms. In addition to an essential thread of nonviolence that also runs through the tale (most notably in the repeated sparing of Gollum's life), Tolkien's trilogy provides us with a timely myth about social engagement. When Frodo leaves home, it is not to slay a dragon or win some treasure but to *let go* of something. His renunciation of the Ring is not done for any selfish purpose but to save the world—the defining characteristic of a bodhisattva. Moreover, the "karmic structure" of Middle-earth (namely, that good intentions lead to good results, while evil intentions are self-defeating) suggests that karma need not be understood as some inevitable calculus of moral cause and effect, as a teaching about how to control what the world does to us. Rather, karma is about our own spiritual development: how

our lives are transformed when we transform the motivations of our actions. Karma is not something I *have*. It is what I *am*, and what I am is changed by what I choose to do, even as Frodo is changed by what he chooses to do.

The Ring shows this. Gollum may think he uses it freely, but using it transforms him. It corrupts anyone who uses it. The Ring of Power also highlights the challenge for engaged Buddhism. Traditional Buddhism has not had much to say about power, but today the root social problem seems to be the individual and collective craving for power (or money, which can be understood as "congealed" power). This craved-for power tends to destroy whatever it touches and whoever is infected by it, as happened to Midas. Lust for it motivates the greed, ill will, and delusions that drive the plot in *The Lord of the Rings*. Tolkien shows us the suffering that results from a quest for power lacking morality; Buddhism emphasizes the suffering that results from seeking or wielding power without wisdom and compassion. In contrast to the imperialistic, militaristic, and technological will to power expressed by Sauron and Saruman, Frodo and the rest of the Fellowship feel no need to dominate Middle-earth. For them it is enough to be a part of Middle-earth, because it is their home. We may need to recover their sensibility if we are to make it through the darkness that has begun to descend on our world.

The German writer Michael Ende is better known for *The Neverending Story*, another classic fantasy, but *Momo* makes a more pointed, Zen-like critique of our obsession with time. What would life be like if we could actually deposit extra time in a Time Bank, akin to the way we deposit money? That provocative notion allows Ende to exaggerate our preoccupation with saving time, to reveal why time cannot be saved and what we lose when we try to do so. The world of the eponymous title character, a homeless street child, is turned upside down when mysterious gray men start persuading people to deposit their saved time in the Timesaving Bank. As Momo's friends become caught up in the general rush to save time, life for everyone becomes hurried and fraught. When she discovers who the gray men really are and what they are doing with all that saved time, Momo decides to take them on, with the assistance of a magical tortoise and Professor Secundus Minutus Hora.

Chapter 3, "The Dharma of Time," offers a Buddhist reading of this charming fable with the help of a thirteenth-century Japanese Zen master. Dogen's *Shobogenzo* offers some of the most insightful Buddhist reflections on the dualism we usually experience between ourselves and the objective, external time we are "in." That delusive duality is not real but mentally constructed, which means it can be deconstructed. Dogen undoes it by demonstrating that things *are* time and, conversely, that time *is* things. That is also true of us. We are not *in* time because we *are* time—which is why we cannot save time. When we try to do so, instead of gaining something we just lose the here-and-now.

The acclaimed Japanese *anime* master Hayao Miyazaki has directed many classic films that deserve to be better known outside Japan, but two of them are particularly fascinating because they offer a Buddhist-like perspective on what has been called the "myth of redemptive violence." Chapter 4, "The Dharma of Nonviolence,"

3 1833 04750 9002

develops that perspective by discussing and comparing *Nausicaa of the Valley of the Winds* and *Princess Mononoke*. While highlighting the destructive effects of human society on nature, both storylines are motivated by hatred and revenge, which different groups use to rationalize their violence against others. Both plots challenge the assumption that violence is an acceptable way to resolve conflict, and both depict an alternative that questions our usual duality between good (us) and evil (them).

For Buddhism, too, the duality between good and evil is another example of delusive thinking. We distinguish between them because we prefer one to the other, but we cannot have one without the other: the meaning of each depends upon (denying) its opposite. In the case of good versus evil, the temptation is to demonize the *other* in order to feel that *we* are good. To stop the self-defeating cycle of violence that results, *Nausicaa* and *Mononoke* both point toward a more insightful distinction between what might be called two modes of being in the world. We can either try to control our world, to make it less threatening, or open ourselves up to the world, which involves letting go of the need to dominate it. Fear or love: the basic choice that confronts each of us.

In Chapter 5, "The Dharma of Death and Life," the fear of death—a constant but submerged theme in the previous chapters—becomes the main focus as we turn to two fantasy series that climax with remarkably similar visits to the Land of the Dead, both of which involve liberating the dead from death. Philip Pullman's *His Dark Materials* trilogy turns the Biblical story of Adam and Eve's Fall upside down, in order to criticize religious superstition and repression.

His two main characters are Lyra and Will, children from different dimensions who travel to a Hades-like afterworld where harpies torment the ghostly shades of the dead, by constantly reminding them of all the bad and stupid things they did while they were alive. Created by a despicable "God," the afterlife turns out to be an endless purgatory without any possibility of expiation. Will uses his magic knife to cut a "window" into another world, yet the dead who step into that world dissolve back into the elements that compose them, something most of them are nevertheless eager to do. Life and death, Pullman implies, should not be seen as opposites. To live we must embrace both. Repressing the fear of our inevitable death casts a shadow over our life. To be unable to die is to be unable to live. This suggests a possible solution: perhaps we can learn how to live by learning how to die, by letting go of ourselves right now. *Satori,* the term for enlightenment in Japanese Zen, is sometimes called the Great Death.

Ursula K. Le Guin's *Earthsea* books are set in an island world where institutionalized magic serves much the same role as modern technology for us. The main character in the first three novels is Ged, a young boy training as a wizard who eventually becomes the Archmage. His first visit to the afterworld occurs before he is mature enough, and ends up releasing a horrible shadow into Earthsea, which haunts and attacks Ged until he confronts it and becomes one with it, in the realization that it is his own death. A later visit to the same afterworld—like Pullman's, a Hades-like realm of sad, staring ghosts without passion or hope—is in response to the failing Equilibrium that threatens Earthsea. The problem is caused by another mage who has managed to gain immortality by rupturing a barrier between the worlds of the living and the dead. Ged shows Cob that death is the price of our life and all life, and that his immortality is a hollow nothingness that can never be filled. With great difficulty, and at the cost of his own powers, Ged is able to close the hole between the worlds.

In the final and most memorable novel, Ged plays a minor role, but the whole series climaxes in the shocking realization that the timeless realm of the afterworld was originally created by wizards unable to accept their own mortality. The dead, we learn again, yearn not for life but for death: to rejoin and become one with the earth again. At the conclusion, a stone wall separating the living from the dead is knocked down, and—just as in Pullman's climax—the dead cross that barrier to dissolve and return to the earth, to be reborn in various ways as different beings.

Buddhism also denies that wall, and the Middle Path gives us another way to break it down. For Dogen too, birth and death are not opposites, and his *Shobogenzo* emphasizes that we should not seek a liberation that involves transcending them. Rather, we need to realize that birth is no-birth, death is no-death. Birth is not something that leads to death, and death is not something that birth has led to. If there is no self that is living, there is only the process of living. And if there is no self that dies, then there is only the process of dying. When our final, dying gasps are whole and complete in themselves, because there is nothing to gain or lose, then our own death becomes no-death. Death loses its sting in "just *this*!" (*tada* in Japanese, *tathata* in Sanskrit).

By no coincidence, all the stories discussed in this book are fantasies aimed especially at children and young adults, who can appreciate and benefit from them without necessarily understanding them intellectually. As adults, most of us eventually settle, comfortably or not, into a constructed world that we accept as reality; children are more open to the possibilities that fantasy expresses imaginatively—alternatives that offer a very different perspective on our world. The best fantasies depict people and situations in ways that we find strange yet still basically familiar. Like the warped images reflected by a carnival mirror, their exaggerated realities reflect and highlight something about the human condition. The Lord of the Rings is set in a Middle-earth largely derived from the Nordic and Germanic mythologies of northern Europe, but Frodo's selfless quest nevertheless provides a model for the socially engaged spirituality we need in our world today. Momo starts out on the fringes of a modern Italian-like city, but soon slips into a world where time can be saved like money and gray men live by smoking it up, a clever conceit that is used to expose our own preoccupation with saving time. Both of Miyazaki's films gain their perspective on this world by being placed in distant times. In Nausicaa's post-apocalyptic future, military holocaust and ecological collapse have left the earth poisoned and fragmented into warring tribes, while Mononoke is set at that critical moment in the medieval past when villages are learning how to exploit nature in order to make iron. In both cases environmental destruction provides the context for plots that expose and challenge the myth of redemptive violence (the belief that aggression is the way to purify the world of its evil) embedded and cherished in so many of our other stories. As a way to challenge the dualisms and repressions of Western religious consciousness, Pullman's trilogy is set in a "multiverse" (a multi-dimensional universe) where windows can be cut between countless worlds, one of them ours and some others similar to ours. And Le Guin's *Earthsea* series takes place in a seafaring world where magic serves as technology—ultimately, with the same baneful consequences.

Of course, there are many other fantasies that offer us more than entertainment. The ones discussed in this book are valuable because they reveal something important about the real world, even as this world for many of us has become a fantasy. According to Buddhism, *samsara*—this world, our world—is not only full of suffering and craving, it is a realm of delusion. The problem is deeper than the ignorance and indifference now cultivated by "infotainment" disguised as news. To understand it, we need only look at the most popular stories today: that is, the stories we consume and live by, which therefore karmically consume and try to live through us.

Many of us now live in a fantasy world where the actualities of our own daily lives are less meaningful than the larger-than-life images that dance on big screens and small boxes. Reality has been turned inside out: the attractive, self-assured media personalities we watch are more real than we are, the rest of us having become bit players in their drama. Television does not reflect reality, it determines it. From watching so many films and TV stories, we have learned to think that life has, or should have, the same narrative structure: beautiful people get the main roles; it is always obvious who the bad guys are; violence is necessary to resolve conflict and it works just fine; what is most valuable in life is physical prowess, sexual attraction, and wit; the really important issue is whether to have sex with someone; and good guys deserve to consume—er, live—happily ever after. We consume these stories and want to live them ourselves, and we are disappointed when this myth does not want to become our reality.

Of course, we really know the difference between television/movies and real life...or do we? Why was the draft dodger John Wayne awarded a Congressional Medal of Honor? He was never a hero, but he played one in enough movies until he eventually became one in the eyes of many. Ronald Reagan, the "acting president," was another notable beneficiary of our collective inability to distinguish image from reality, and more recently the people of California have chosen a cinematic cyborg to be their governor—although he seems to have no qualifications whatsoever for the job except that his films have conditioned us to believe that he must be a hero.

There are many variations on such media-induced collective fantasies, of course. For men, especially, there is the annual cycle of professional and collegiate sports. It is a safe bet that more men know who won the Superbowl or World Series than can identify their representative in the U.S. Congress. Yet it really does not matter who wins the championship; it is meaningless in the sense that it has no significance outside itself. It is a story whose only function is to absorb our excess time and attention, and provide a venue for advertising. Some people see through these fantasies only to fall into an older one, the classical American myth of the tough, self-made, self-sufficient individual looking out for Number One, a perspective often influenced by vague social Darwinist stories about the survival of the fittest.

To wake up from such samsaric myths, which tend to reinforce our ignorance, craving, and therefore our suffering, we recommend—in addition to the Middle Path—the insightful and liberative myths of Tolkien, Ende, Miyazaki, Pullman, and Le Guin.

Of course, the Buddhist perspectives that follow are no substitute for reading (or viewing, in the case of Miyazaki's *anime*) the original fantasies themselves. As particularly excellent examples of contemporary spiritual myth, they deserve to be appreciated without being filtered through our Buddhist take on them. If you have not yet experienced these stories yourself, we hope that the following chapters will encourage you to do so. Personal familiarity will place you in a better position to understand, and reflect upon, how profoundly Buddhist these fantasies are.

.

.

.

.

.

.

.

.

Pickup Before: 7/18/2017

DEKORSEY

6470

2

The Dharma of
Engagement

J. R. R. Tolkien's
The Lord of the Rings

I sometimes feel appalled at the thought of the sum total of human misery all over the world at the present moment: the millions parted, fretting, wasting in unprofitable days—quite apart from torture, pain, death, bereavement, injustice. If anguish were visible, almost the whole of this benighted planet would be enveloped in a dense dark vapor, shrouded from the amazed vision of the heavens! And the products of it all will be mainly evil—historically considered. But the historic version is, of course, not the only one. All things and deeds have a value in themselves, apart from their "causes" and "effects." No man can estimate what is really happening at the moment sub specie aeternitas. All we do know, and that to a large extent by direct experience, is that evil labors with vast power and perpetual success—in vain: preparing always only the soil for unexpected good to sprout in. So it is in general, and so it is in our own lives.

—J. R. R. Tolkien to his son Christopher,
30 April 1944[3]

HE LORD OF THE RINGS as a modern Buddhist myth? Not very plausible, on the face of it. As is well known, Middle-earth is derived largely from the Nordic and Germanic sagas that Tolkien knew so well. Although neither God nor a Redeemer is ever mentioned, the tale expresses some Christian influence, according to Tolkien's own admission (he was a devout Roman Catholic)—for example, the sacrificial death and resurrection of Gandalf. There is no hint, either in the story or in its sources, of any Buddhist influences.

Moreover, Tolkien's fantasy world is built on a radical and quite un-Buddhist dualism between unredeemable evil (Sauron, Saruman) and uncompromising goodness (Gandalf, Frodo). The good as well as the bad use violence in pursuit of their goals, and we are entertained with plenty of it. Stupid and cruel as they may be, orcs remain sentient beings. From a Buddhist perspective, therefore, they must have the same buddha-nature as all other living beings, with the potential to "wake up" from their greed, ill will and delusion. Bodhisattvas vow to "save" all sentient beings, in the sense of helping them to realize their true nature. In Middle-earth, though, no one has any interest in helping orcs awaken. The only good orc is a dead orc, and in the battle of Helm's Deep, Gimli and Legolas cheerfully compete to see who can kill more. Gimli wins with forty-two victims of his ax, one more than those dispatched by Legolas's arrows.

And yet...Tolkien's masterpiece achieves what he intended, which was to create a modern myth; and myths, as he also knew, have a way of growing beyond their creator's intentions. *The Lord of the Rings* is much more than an endearing fantasy about little hobbits, gruff dwarves, and light-footed elves. It has been repeatedly voted the novel of the century—according to some, it is the novel of the millennium!—because so many readers find it deeply moving as well. What is it about the tale that makes it so compelling, so *mythic?* One answer, for us at least, is that despite its European origins it resonates with Buddhist concerns and perspectives.

Evil, for example, is much more nuanced than it appears at first glance. "In my story I do not deal with Absolute Evil. I do not think there is such a thing, since that is Zero" (*L* 243). As Gandalf reminds the Fellowship, "Nothing is evil in the beginning. Even Sauron was not so." Sauron too was corrupted, long ago, by his craving for the Ring. It is no coincidence that, as the foremost expression of evil, he is never seen (only his hand and "eye rimmed with fire"). Sauron is more effective as an abstract principle, so malignant and powerful that he could not be depicted as a believable person. The implication, in Buddhist terms, is that evil, too, has no self-being. Like everything else, it is a result of causes and conditions that we allow to infect and defile our minds.

There is also an essential, Buddhist-like thread of nonviolence that runs throughout the tale. Despite all the bloodshed, a repeated act of compassion—sparing Gollum's life—is crucial to the plot. Early in the story, when Frodo comments that it was a pity Bilbo did not stab Gollum when he had a chance, Gandalf contradicts him: "Pity? It was Pity that stayed his hand. Pity; and Mercy: not to strike without need. And he has been well rewarded, Frodo. Be sure that he took so little result from the evil, and escaped in the end, because he began his ownership of the Ring so. With Pity" (*FR* 89). It is important for Frodo's quest that he learns this lesson. Much later, when Faramir is about to have Gollum killed, Frodo intercedes at the risk of his own life: "Let me go down quietly to him....You may keep your bows bent and shoot me, at least, if I fail. I shall not run away" (*TT* 368). At the very end, when Frodo and his company have returned to the Shire and saved it from Sharkey's men, Frodo intercedes when the other hobbits want to kill Sharkey (formerly Saruman): "I will not have him slain. It is useless to meet revenge with revenge: it will heal nothing. Go, Saruman, by the speediest way!" (*RK* 363).

There is virtually no role for religion in Middle-earth, because "the religious element is absorbed into the story and the symbolism" (*L* 172). Nevertheless, *The Lord of the Rings* can serve as a Buddhist fable because it is about a spiritual quest readily understandable in terms of the teachings of Buddhism. Despite Tolkien's demurral that it has "any meaning or 'message'" (*FR* 11), his tale provides a myth about spiritual engagement for modern Buddhists. Frodo leaves home not to slay a dragon or win a chest full of precious jewels, but to *let go* of something, which is what one learns to do with one's ego-centered view of the world when following the Buddhist path. His renunciation of the Ring is not done to gain enlightenment, yet it nonetheless transforms him spiritually. The suffering he experiences on the way to Mount Doom deepens him, making him stronger and more compassionate. However, Frodo's journey does more than illustrate the traditional Buddhist path. It teaches us how karma works and even helps us to understand

Buddhism today. Karma is often understood as a law that operates mechanically, but perhaps it functions in a more subtle psychological way.

The way Tolkien wrote *The Lord of the Rings* also has something to teach us. Tolkien's rather uneventful life as a English don is well known and does not need to be recounted here, nor does the plot require retelling. However, the intersection between them—the manner in which he composed his fantasy—highlights something important about the nature of creativity: *it is not the "self" that creates.* Tolkien's descriptions of his own experience echo what many great (and some not-so-great) authors have attested to: the story wrote itself. The stories "arose in my mind as 'given' things...yet always I had the sense of recording what was already 'there,' somewhere: not of 'inventing'" (*L 145*). In 1938–39 "*The Lord of the Rings* was beginning to unroll itself and to unfold prospects of labour and exploration in yet unknown country as daunting to me as to the hobbits. At the same time we had reached Bree, and I had then no more notion than they had what had become of Gandalf or who Strider was; and I had begun to despair of surviving to find out."[4] Much later, a letter to the poet W. H. Auden reveals more understanding of the process, or more patience with it:

> "I have long ceased to *invent*.... I wait till I seem to know what really happened. Or till it writes itself...."
>
> Strider sitting in the corner at the inn was a shock, and I had no more idea who he was than had Frodo. The Mines of Moria had been a mere name; and of Lothlorien no word had reached my mortal ears till I came

there. Far away I knew there were the Horse-lords on the confines of an ancient Kingdom of Men, but Fangorn Forest was an unforeseen adventure. I had never heard of the House of Eorl nor of the Stewards of Gondor. Most disquieting of all, Saruman had never been revealed to me, and I was as mystified as Frodo at Gandalf's failure to appear on September 22. I knew nothing of the Palantiri, though the moment the Orthanc-stone was cast from the window, I recognized it. (*L* 231, 216–17)

Such creation involves openness to a source that is other than, and more than, one's own sense of self. It is, arguably, a *spiritual process* consistent with Tolkien's intention to create a myth that might speak to our modern condition, because it would explore and suggest answers to some of our deepest problems and questions. He once mentioned to a friend that he was concerned that the English had so few myths of their own, "so I thought I'd make one myself." That offhand remark disguises the seriousness of his mythopoetic project. In Tolkien's view, his contemporaries "had forgotten that the mythological imagination could deal in a profoundly revelatory way with serious moral and spiritual issues. He himself had learned, through the creation of his mythological realm of Middle-earth, something new and yet very old—that a living mythology can deepen rather than cloud our vision of reality."[5]

Humphrey Carpenter's biography of Tolkien gives an account of a legendary 1931 conversation with C.S. Lewis. Lewis, not yet a Christian, was insisting that myths are lies, "even though lies breathed through silver." No, replied Tolkien: we come from God, and the myths created by us, although they inevitably include some error, nevertheless "reflect a splintered fragment of the true light, the eternal truth that is with God." It is only through our myth-making, in which we become a "sub-creator" inventing stories, that we can aspire to the perfection humans knew before the Fall. Although our myths may be inadequate, they steer us, however precariously, toward the true harbor, while the materialistic alternative called "progress" leads only to the abyss that crowns the power of evil.[6] Tolkien repeated this in a 1951 letter: "I believe that legends and myths are largely made of 'truth,' and indeed present aspects of it that can only be received in this mode; and long ago certain truths and modes of this kind were discovered and must always reappear" (*L* 147).

Carpenter considers this to be Tolkien's central philosophy, echoing throughout his writings. It is crucial to Tolkien's other major work, *The Silmarillion*, in which the Two Trees that illuminate the world's creation are destroyed. Their luminosity survives in the Silmarilli, three jewels that form part of Morgoth's Iron Crown. Later those gems are also lost and their own light splinters, leaving only mythic fragments and memories in Middle-earth by the time of the events that occur in *The Lord of the Rings*.

If splintered light from the Silmarilli still survives today, it is not easy to find. We have plenty of stories, more than ever before, but most of them are escapist literature that does not inspire us with any vision of what we are to do and what we might become. It is no coincidence, Tolkien believed, that despite our Promethean projects, modern self-esteem—our collective self-image—is probably lower and more degraded than ever. "A hero is the expression of a culture's ideals about itself, and our ideals about ourselves have all been punctured."[7] Tolkien argued that in contrast to what we now call the "mind candy" of most bestsellers, fantasy can occasionally still give us a glimpse into something "higher": Divinity itself, in his Christian understanding, or, in Buddhist terms, buddha-nature, which is nothing other than our own essential nature. In a 1938 lecture, "On Fairy-Stories," he claimed that such stories can bring "a sudden and miraculous grace" that gives "a fleeting glimpse of Joy, Joy beyond the walls of the world"—something indistinguishable, in effect, from spiritual experience. He coined the term "eucatastrophe" to describe the sudden happy turn in a story that pierces us with a joy bringing tears to our eyes: "And I was there led to the view that it produces its peculiar effect because it is a sudden glimpse of Truth, your whole nature chained in material cause and effect, the chain of death, feels a sudden relief as if a major limb out of joint had suddenly snapped back. It perceives—if the story has 'literary truth' on the second plane—that this is indeed how things really do work in the Great World for which our nature is made." (L 100).

Mythology can help us regain the freshness of vision that he called "recovery." This is a recuperation readily understandable to Buddhists, whose meditation practices also involve restoring a "clear view" of the world "so that the things seen clearly may be freed from the drab blur of triteness and familiarity." This is not only a renewal of health but the healing of a spiritual blindness.[8]

How well does Tolkien's own fantasy capture the dimmed light of the shattered Silmarilli? And how well can his Nordic-influenced,

Christian-inspired fantasy speak to the mythological needs of Buddhists today?

An Engaged Quest

From a socially-engaged Buddhist perspective, concerned to bring Buddhist teachings to bear on contemporary social issues, one of the striking aspects of the plot is that Frodo does not *want* to have the adventures he has. He embarks on the quest because it cannot be evaded. At the beginning Sam is excited about going to "see elves and all," but Frodo is more apprehensive, and for good reason. The Ring must be destroyed and he is the best one to carry it. In some mysterious, inexplicable way the task has been appointed to him. There is nothing he hopes to gain from the journey. By the end, he and Sam expect to be destroyed themselves soon after the Ring is cast into the Chamber of Fire, and indeed they nearly are. Their total renunciation is a powerful metaphor for Buddhist practice. As practitioners, we are sometimes willing to give up everything for enlightenment—but that is the catch. It is the *self* that seeks to be enlightened, that still wants to be around to enjoy being enlightened. Self remains the problem. Frodo and Sam show us something deeper. They let go of all personal ambition, although not the ambition to do what is necessary to help others. In Buddhist terms, they become bodhisattvas.

Frodo's quest is not an attempt to transcend Middle-earth by realizing some higher reality or dimension. He is simply responding to its needs, which, because of historical circumstances (the growing power of Sauron, now actively seeking the Ring), have become critical—as are the needs of our beleaguered earth today. The larger world has begun to impinge on his Shire (and ours). If Frodo were to decline the task and hide at home, he would not escape the dangers that threaten. The Dark Lord would soon discover him and his Ring, and the Shire along with the rest of Middle-earth would fall under his baneful control. When we consider the ecological and social crises that have begun to impinge on our own little worlds, is our situation any different?

So is Frodo's journey a spiritual quest or a struggle to help the world? In *The Lord of the Rings* these two are the same. Frodo realizes ("makes real") his own nonduality with the world by doing everything he can to help it. Middle-earth needs to be *saved*, not denied or escaped. (Contrast the secret wardrobe that leads to a very different world in C.S. Lewis's *Narnia* books—works that Tolkien disliked because of their blatant allegory.) The goal is not another world but another way of living in this one, even as nirvana is not another place but a liberated way of experiencing this one. In the process, Frodo learns that this world is very different from what he thought it was. And by doing what he can to transform it, Frodo transforms himself. That is how his selflessness is developed. Frodo does not change because he destroys the Ring. He changes because of his tireless efforts to destroy the Ring. His early adventures on the road to Rivendell challenge and toughen him, giving him the courage to be the Ringbearer. His own strength of heart and will grow from those encounters, teaching him initiative and perseverance, and eventually developing into his unassuming heroic stature.

Gandalf cannot accompany Frodo and Sam all the way. The plot dramatically requires him to fall away, so that Frodo and Sam can mature further into the role they need to play. Gandalf sacrifices himself defending his colleagues and disappears to undergo his own psychic death and resurrection. Appropriately, that occurs deep in the dark mines of Moria. Is the same true for our own spiritual paths? No matter how wise and compassionate our teachers may be, they cannot walk the path for us. As our meditations take us down into the dark unconscious of our own minds, we disturb our own deepest fears and must face them ourselves. And we too do not enter that underground world willingly. Our quest takes us there—usually driven to it by the failures of our lives, by our *dukkha* suffering.

The Karma of the Rings

Middle-earth is a morally balanced world. As Randel Helms has pointed out, the essential law of Tolkien's story is that good intentions lead to good results, while evil intentions end up being self-defeating.[9] In Buddhist terms, we could say that Middle-earth is structured karmically: the way the main characters in Middle-earth act becomes the way Middle-earth responds to them. What they put out comes back to help or haunt them. This Buddhist-like principle of moral causation is one of the keys to the plot, recurring again and again.

It is easy enough to see how good intentions are rewarded, but the negative consequences of bad intentions are just as important to the success of Frodo and Sam's mission. For example, consider the effects of Boromir's attempt to seize the Ring from Frodo by the river Anduin. He wants to help save Gondor, yet deceiving the others and taking the Ring by force would be disastrous for everyone. Boromir's unsuccessful effort is quickly followed by his expiatory death, defending the hobbits against an orc attack, but it also leads to Frodo's decision to set out alone for Mordor. This breaking-up of the Fellowship is needed in order for Merry and Pippin to meet Treebeard and play their part in destroying Isengard, and it is also necessary for Aragorn to play his vital role in the battles to come:

> "Let me think!" said Aragorn. "And now may I make a right choice, and change the evil fate of this unhappy day!" He stood silent for a moment. "I will follow the Orcs," he said at last. "I would have guided Frodo to Mordor and gone with him to the end; but if I seek him now in the wilderness, I must abandon the captives to torment and death. My heart speaks clearly at last: the fate of the Bearer is in my hands no longer." (TT 19)

Aragorn's decision to chase the orcs who have seized Merry and Pippin leads to many unintended positive consequences, including meeting Eomer and Gandalf, that also turn out to be important for the fulfillment of the quest.

Another example of a bad intention defeating itself is Wormtongue hurling the powerful *palantir* globe out of the window of Saruman's besieged Orthanc. It is apparently aimed at Gandalf but glances off an iron railing and rolls along the ground, to be retrieved by Pippin. This ill-tempered gesture is another crucial mistake, for in the hands of Pippin and then Aragorn the *palantir* not only removes Saruman's means of contacting Sauron but helps to distract Sauron's attention from the Ringbearers who are approaching Mordor. As Gandalf reflects:

> "Strange are the turns of fortune! Often does hatred hurt itself! I guess that, even if we had entered it, we could have found few treasures in Orthanc more precious than the thing which Wormtongue threw down at us."
>
> A shrill shriek, suddenly cut off, came from an open window high above.
>
> "It seems that Saruman thinks so too," said Gandalf. (*TT* 237)

King Theoden sums it up best in the inevitable aphorism: "Strange powers have our enemies, and strange weaknesses! But it has long been said: *oft evil will shall evil mar*" (*TT* 250).

The best example of self-defeating evil motivation is, of course, Gollum. He does not want to help Frodo and Sam. He wants to get his hands on the Ring. To do so, however, he must help them again and again. When they are lost he leads them to Mordor. When they become stuck he shows them a mountain path that leads (through Shelob's tunnel) toward Mount Doom. At the end, when an exhausted Frodo can no longer resist the lure of the Ring, Gollum appears one last time to bite off Frodo's finger—and fall into the fiery pit, to be destroyed along with the Ring. Yet this can happen only because of the compassion toward Gollum repeatedly shown by Frodo and eventually by Sam too. Frodo's compassion has already been noticed, but Sam's is just as important. When they are attacked by Gollum while ascending Mount Doom, Frodo fights back furiously and then leaves the cowering Gollum for Sam to deal with.

> Sam's hand wavered. His mind was hot with wrath and the memory of evil. It would be just to slay this treacherous, murderous creature, just and many times deserved; and also it seemed the only safe thing to do. But deep in his heart there was something that restrained him: he could not strike this thing lying in the dust, forlorn, ruinous, utterly wretched. He himself, though only for a little while, had borne the Ring, and now dimly he guessed the agony of Gollum's shriveled mind and body, enslaved to that Ring, unable to find peace or relief ever in life again. (*RK* 267)

This touches on the essence of compassion, and why it is essential to Buddhism: we commiserate with the suffering of another because we share in it, because we are not other than it.

In the Tibetan mandala known as the Wheel of Life, the six realms of samsara are depicted within a circle. At its core are a cock, a snake, and a pig, symbolizing the three poisons of greed, ill will, and delusion, which are the source of all suffering. Curling around them are two paths: on one side, the white upward path of virtue and spiritual development, on the other, the dark downward path of evil and its painful consequences. *The Lord of the Rings* illustrates both alternatives in the moral progress and deserved rewards of Frodo, Sam, Aragorn, and Gandalf, and in the utter failure and eventual destruction of Sauron, Gollum, Saruman, and Wormtongue.

In Middle-earth this karmic law works as inexorably as gravity, but, as we know all too well, karma does not operate so neatly in our world—at least, not in the short run. Evil often seems to succeed; goodness has a harder time prevailing. "Here is perhaps the basic difference between the moral structures of Tolkien's world and our own. We know that intention has nothing to do with result."[10] According to Buddhism, however, intention has a lot to do with results in our world too, for intention is the heart of karma. But if, as religious scholars often point out, religious language should usually be taken metaphorically, Buddhist teachings about karma can be and perhaps should be understood less literally than they usually are.

On our earth as in Middle-earth, it is clear that karma does not mean all events are predestined to happen. Some inexplicable destiny has given Frodo responsibility for the Ring, as Gandalf and Elrond realize, yet what he does with it depends upon his own decisions. His success is not preordained. In both worlds karma creates situations but does not determine how we respond to them.

There is, however, much more to say about what karma is and how it works. Karma and rebirth have become a problem for modern Buddhists that cannot be evaded. To accept what the earliest Buddhist teachings say about them as literal truth, as most Buddhists throughout history seem to have done, leads to a severe case of cognitive dissonance for contemporary Buddhism. The physical causality that modern science has discovered about the world seems to allow no mechanism for karma or rebirth to operate. There is no empirically-verifiable evidence to support either of them as a law of the universe. This means that if we choose to combine scientific laws of causality with a commitment to not-scientifically-supported but equally impersonal, objective laws of moral reciprocity, as many modern Buddhists try to do, we end up with a kind of intellectual and spiritual schizophrenia that the Buddha himself certainly did not encourage.

In the Kalama Sutra, sometimes called "the Buddhist charter of free inquiry," the Buddha emphasized the importance of intelligent, probing doubt. We should not believe in something until we know its truth for ourselves. For us to believe in karmic rebirth in a literal way, simply because it is part of the Buddhist teaching (or part of the way that the Buddha's teaching has traditionally been understood), may thus be unfaithful to the best of the tradition. This is not to deny the *possibility* of a truth that we cannot confirm. The point is that our modern ways of knowing offer no support for those teachings, and given a healthy skepticism about the Iron Age belief systems of the Buddha's time, we should hesitate before making such a leap of faith. Maybe rebirth according to one's karma is literally true as an explanation of what happens after we physically die. However, it may not be true. Instead of tying our spiritual paths to belief in such a doctrine, isn't it wiser for us to be agnostic about it?

But challenging a literal understanding is not to dismiss or disparage Buddhist teachings about karma and rebirth. Rather, it highlights the need for modern Buddhism to *interrogate* them. Given what is now known about human psychology, including the social construction of the self, how can karma and rebirth be understood today?

During the time of Shakyamuni Buddha, karma and reincarnation were widely although not universally accepted religious principles. They were part of the cultural milieu within which he grew up. Earlier teachings such as the Vedas tended to understand them more mechanically and ritualistically. To perform a sacrifice in the proper fashion would invariably lead to the desired consequences. If those consequences were not forthcoming, then either there had been an error in procedure or the causal effects were delayed, perhaps until one's next lifetime. The Buddha's spiritual revolution transformed this ritualistic approach to controlling one's life into an ethical principle by emphasizing our *motivations*.

Experiences are preceded by mind, led by mind, and produced by mind. If one speaks or acts with an impure mind, suffering follows even as the cart-wheel follows the hoof of the ox.

Experiences are preceded by mind, led by mind, and produced by mind. If one speaks or acts with a pure mind, happiness follows like a shadow that never departs.[11]

Here it may be helpful to distinguish a moral act into its three aspects: our *motivation* when we do something, the *moral rule* (for example, a Buddhist precept or Christian commandment) we are following, and the *results* that we seek. These aspects cannot be separated from each other, but we can emphasize one more than the others—in fact, that is what we usually do.[12] In the Buddha's time, the Brahmanical understanding of karma emphasized the importance of following the detailed procedures (rules) regulating each ritual; naturally, however, the people who paid for the rituals were more interested in the outcome (results). Arguably, the situation in some Theravada countries is not much different today: monastics are preoccupied with following the complicated rules regulating their lives, while many laypeople are eager to accumulate merit by giving gifts to them. Unfortunately, this arrangement amounts to a return to Brahmanism that loses the Buddha's great insight about the preeminent importance of our motivations. How should we today understand the originality of his approach?

Karma need not be viewed as some inevitable calculus of moral cause and effect, because it is not primarily a teaching about how to control what the world does to us. It is about our own spiritual development: how our lives are transformed by our motivations. When we add the Buddhist teaching about nonself—the claim, consistent with modern psychology, that one's sense of self is a mental construct—we can say that karma is not something I *have*, it is what I *am*, and what I am changes according to what I choose to do. "I" (re)construct myself by what I intentionally do. My sense of self is a precipitate of my habitual ways of thinking, feeling, and acting. Just as my body is composed of the food I eat, so my character is composed of my conscious choices, constructed by my consistent, repeated motivations. People are "punished" or "rewarded" not for what they have done but for what they have become, and what we intentionally do is what makes us what we are. A familiar anonymous verse expresses this well:

Sow a thought and reap a deed.

Sow a deed and reap a habit.

Sow a habit and reap a character.

Sow a character and reap a destiny.

Such an understanding of karma does not necessarily involve another life after we physically die. As Spinoza expressed it, happiness is not the reward for virtue; happiness is virtue itself. To become a different kind of person is to experience the world in a different way. When your mind changes, the world changes. (This is nothing new to those who have taken psychedelic drugs: affecting one's brain chemistry transforms the way one experiences the "external" world.) And when we respond differently to the world, the world responds differently to us. Since we are actually nondual with the world—our sense of separation from it being a delusion—our ways of acting in it tend to involve reinforcing feedback systems that incorporate other people. People not only notice what we do, they notice why we do it. I may fool people sometimes, but over time my character becomes revealed through the intentions behind my deeds. The more I am motivated by greed, ill will, and delusion, the more I must manipulate the world to get what I want, and consequently the more alienated I feel and the more alienated others feel when they see they have been manipulated. This mutual distrust encourages both sides to manipulate more. Saruman and Wormtongue exemplify this cycle of negative feedback. On the other hand, the more my actions are motivated by generosity, loving-kindness, and the wisdom of nonduality, the more I can relax and open up to the world.

The more I feel part of the world and at one with others, the less I am inclined to use others, and consequently the more inclined they will be to trust and open up to me. Frodo and Sam's encounter with Faramir is an example of such positive feedback.

Consistent with this view of karma, the traditional "six realms" of samsara do not need to be distinct worlds or planes of existence through which we transmigrate after death, according to our karma. They can also be the different ways we experience this world, as our character, and therefore our attitude toward the world, change. For example, the hell realm becomes not so much a place I will be reborn into later, due to my hatred and evil deeds, as a way I experience this world when my mind is dominated by anger and hate.

The Karma of Power

What is the Ring? Its magnetic attraction is a profound symbol for the karma of power. We think we use the Ring, but when we use it, it is actually using us, *it changes us*—this is the essential karmic insight. Power corrupts, and the absolute power of the Ring corrupts absolutely. At the end even Frodo cannot resist it, as he stands exhausted before the Crack of Doom.

Power wants to be used. "A Ring of Power looks after itself, Frodo. *It* may slip off treacherously, but its keeper never abandons it" (*FR* 83). The Ring has a will of its own. It gets heavier. It wants Frodo to slip it on his finger. If he were to do this, though, it would corrupt him, as it corrupted Sauron and Gollum long ago. Gollum is Frodo's alter ego, a constant reminder to Frodo of what he could become.

Power is eager to test and display itself. What is the point of having an overwhelming military machine if you don't use it once in a while? When you create a new weapon (for example, a "smart" bomb), you want to see what it can do in a combat situation. The scientists who created the first nuclear bombs during the Second World War, all the while hoping these weapons would not be needed, learned about this the hard way. Once the bombs had been made, their own wishes were of no consequence. But is there something more to learn from the Ring of Power?

Buddhism has not had much to say about power. Traditional teachings warn more about sex and other physical cravings, which play almost no role in *The Lord of the Rings*. The absolute prohibition of sexual contact for monastics suggests that sexual desire is the archetypal craving that needs to be transcended in order to achieve the serenity of nirvana. Whether or not that was true in India 2,500 years ago, our situation calls for a different focus. Today the primary challenge for socially engaged Buddhism is the individual and collective craving for power, which Midas-like destroys whatever it touches. Power and money may be quite valuable as *means* to some good end, but they turn destructive when they become *ends* in themselves. Sauron and Saruman, like Gollum, no longer have any goal but power itself—the power that is the Ring. With them Tolkien shows the suffering that results from a quest for power lacking a moral dimension.

In *The Lord of the Rings* lust for power motivates the greed, ill will, and delusion that drive the plot. Sauron rules a totalitarian and imperialistic state. Saruman transforms his domain into a fearsome military machine. According to Treebeard, "He has a mind of metal and wheels; and he does not care for growing things, except as far as they serve him for the moment" (*TT* 90). Defeated, Saruman slinks off to the Shire, where, as Sharkey, he introduces an ecologically destructive industrial revolution that begins to turn it into a wasteland like the area around Isengard. Hobbit holes are replaced with brick slums and factories. His new mills, full of wheels and outlandish contraptions, are "always a-hammering and a-letting out a smoke and a stench, and there isn't no peace even at night in Hobbiton. And they pour out filth a purpose; they've fouled all the lower Water, and it's getting down into Brandywine. If they want to make the Shire into a desert, they're going the right way about it" (*RK* 356).

Sauron, Saruman, and Sharkey are fought and defeated. But are they the same thing: different expressions of the will to power over Middle-earth and its creatures?

In contrast, the strength that Gandalf, Aragorn, Frodo, and others demonstrate is shown not by accumulating or exercising power but in their willingness to give it up. Gandalf has no selfish craving for mastery. He wishes only to serve: "The rule of no realm is mine, neither of Gondor nor any other, great or small. But all worthy things that are in peril as the world now stands, those are my care. And for my part, I shall not wholly fail of my task, though Gondor should perish, if anything passes through this night that can still grow fair or bear fruit and flower again in days to come. For I also am a steward" (*RK* 29–30).

Gandalf gives us the definition and the model of a modern bodhisattva, the sort we need today. Are they so rare among us, or is it that the Saurons and Sarumans are so much more visible? And so much more powerful, in the conventional sense, because in our world it is not so much physical craving as lust for power that motivates the greed, ill will, and willful ignorance now endangering the earth. People have always craved power, but because of modern technologies there is now so much more power to crave and use; and because of modern institutions, such power tends to function in impersonal ways that assume a life of their own. Transnational corporations and stock markets institutionalize greed (never enough consumption or profit!) in a world where the centralized bureaucratic governments of nation-states unleash institutionalized ill will (horrific military aggression) in pursuit of their "national interests." Under the guise of globalization, ever more sophisticated technologies are deployed to extend the institutionalized delusion that dualizes us from the earth (by commodifying, exploiting, and laying waste to its furthest corners). Today these institutionalized versions of the three poisons are the Mordor that threatens our future. If Buddhist teachings cannot help us understand this, perhaps there is something wrong with our understanding of Buddhism.

Hobbiton expresses Tolkien's nostalgia for the vanishing rural England in the West Midlands of his youth, but we should not dismiss such homesickness with the reassuring Buddhist maxim that "everything passes away." Our collective attempt to dominate the earth technologically is related to the disappearance of the sacred in the modern world. If we can no longer rely on God to take care of us, we strive to secure ourselves by subduing nature until it meets all our needs and satisfies all our purposes—which will never happen, of course. Because our efforts to exploit the earth's resources are damaging it so much, the fatal irony is that our attempt to secure the conditions of our existence here may destroy us. Is there a clearer or more dangerous example of institutionalized delusion? We are one with the earth. When the biosphere becomes sick, we become sick. If the biosphere dies, we die. The technological Ring of Power is not the solution to our problems. It has become the problem itself.

In contrast to the imperialistic, militaristic, and technological will to power expressed by Sauron and Saruman, Frodo and the rest of the Fellowship share a universal sensibility that has room for many different types of societies. Middle-earth is alive with diverse life-forms—hobbits, elves, dwarves, humans, wizards, ents, orcs—most of whom dwell together, not always peacefully but with a fair degree of harmony, until the shadow of the Dark Lord begins to grow. They feel no need to dominate or commodify Middle-earth. It is enough to be a part of it, because it is home to all of them. Happiness for our heroes is connected with the ability to delight in the simple pleasures of everyday life: enjoying a glass and a song by a warm hearth in the company of others, for example. The fellowship of loving friends is contrasted with the greedy, private pseudo-happiness of those who seek only the Ring. Sauron, Saruman, Gollum: each tormented, solitary soul looks out only for itself, and knows nothing of the wide community of willing helpers that enables Frodo to complete his mission.

We need to recover such community and such an ecological sensibility if we are to make it through the dark times that threaten our world. We also need new types of bodhisattvas, inspired perhaps by the fresh models that Tolkien's myth provides for socially engaged Buddhism. As with Frodo on his improbable quest, it is easy to become discouraged. There is, however, something to remember at such times. Frodo's task was appointed to him in a mysterious way that he did not understand because it cannot be understood. The implication is that the mission he and others undertook was successful in the end because they were a part of something greater than themselves. For us, too, to be spiritual means opening up to a transformative power that works in us and through us when we do the best we can. Is that also true for the world that we are nondual with? Who knows what is possible, or even what is actually happening today? Who, for example, anticipated the worldwide collapse of communism in 1989, or the sudden end of South African apartheid in 1994? The task of socially engaged bodhisattvas is not to unravel the mystery that is our world, but to do what we can to succor its sufferings in this time of crisis. Frodo and Sam discovered many unexpected helpers along their way, and so may we.

The Gift of God to Men

Although not much developed in *The Lord of the Rings*, the rings of power have another function that Tolkien emphasized more in *The Silmarillion* and in his correspondence. As well as making the bearer invisible, the rings provide a poisoned taste of immortality. "The chief power (of all the rings alike) was the prevention or slowing of *decay* (i.e., change, viewed as a regrettable thing), the preservation of what is desired or loved, or its semblance" (*L* 152). Bilbo hardly seems to age during the many years he possesses the Ring. It is the three rings the elves possess that preserve their enchanted enclaves of peace, where time seems to stand still—which is why the destruction of the ruling Ring marks the end of their world.

Prevention of decay points to what Tolkien himself eventually came to regard as the central theme of *The Lord of the Rings*: not power or domination, but fear of death and the desire for immortality. "Though it is only in reading the work myself (with criticisms in mind) that I become aware of the dominance of the theme of Death.... But certainly Death is not an Enemy! I said, or meant to say, that the 'message' was the hideous peril of confusing true 'immortality' with limitless serial longevity. Freedom from Time, and clinging to Time.... The Elves call 'death' the Gift of God (to Men)" (*L* 267).

Desire for immortality plays a major role in *The Silmarillion*, leading to the Downfall of the Second Age. The human Numenoreans dwell within sight of the Eastern paradise Eressea, land of the immortals, yet they are banned from sailing to it. At first they freely accept this prohibition, but eventually, deceived by Sauron's lies, they rebel and decide to break the ban in order to wrest from the gods "everlasting life within the circles of the world." The Numenoreans build an armada to attack the gods. In response, a chasm opens in the sea, engulfing them and also removing the timeless realm of the gods from Middle-earth. This catastrophe ends the old world and leads directly to the Third Age recounted in *The Lord of the Rings.*

Despite Tolkien's increasing interest in death and its implications, this theme remains subordinate in *The Lord of the Rings,* little more than hinted at. From a Buddhist perspective, however, it is a crucial issue. Is there greater psychological suffering than the realization that we and all our loved ones will die within a few years? We return to this topic in the final chapter, for fear of death and desire for immortality become the central concern in Pullman's *His Dark Materials* and Le Guin's *Earthsea.*

3

The Dharma of Time

Michael Ende's *Momo*

The odd thing was, no matter how much time he [Mr. Figaro] saved, he never had any to spare; in some mysterious way, it simply vanished. Imperceptibly at first, but then quite unmistakably, his days grew shorter and shorter.... Something in the nature of a blind obsession had taken hold of him, and when he realized to his horror that his days were flying by faster and faster, as he occasionally did, it only reinforced his grim determination to save time.

—from *Momo*

Today Mr. Figaro's complaint is all too familiar. With so many efficient labor-saving devices, why do we seem to have so much less time? What social scientists call a "time-compression effect" contributes a manic quality to much of daily life. Increased stress, workaholism, sleep deprivation, up to half the U.S. work population suffering from burnout, no leisure for family and friends... something has gone wrong with our time.

Even in 1992, a survey by the U.S. National Recreation and Park Association found that 38 percent of Americans said they "always" felt rushed, up from 22 percent in 1971. More recently Joe Robinson claimed in the *Utne Reader* that the United States has now surpassed Japan as the most overworked country in the industrialized world. He reports that the husband and wife of an average U.S. household are now working 500 more hours a year than they did in 1980. This is an average of 350 hours (nine weeks!) per person more than Europeans.[13] Lou Harris public opinion polls have shown a 37 percent decrease in Americans' reported leisure time over a twenty-year period, leading Harris to assert that "time may have become the most precious commodity in the land."[14]

But what if commodifying time is itself the problem? Perhaps our problem with time is not so different from our problem with everything else. By commodifying we convert things into resources for buying and selling. Today the earth and its beings continue to be commodified in ingenious new ways, such as trading of carbon emission rights and manipulating genetic codes. The industrial revolution transformed life into labor—work time—to be bought and sold, hence time too came to be valued according to supply and demand. Our accelerating postmodern world has aggravated this development. Because we never have enough of it, time has become our most precious resource.

Time as a resource and commodity: what happens if we push that metaphor a little further? We're always trying to save time, so what would life be like if we could actually deposit extra time in a Time Bank, as we do with money? This is precisely the provocative notion developed by Michael Ende in his classic fantasy *Momo*. By exaggerating our preoccupation with saving time, he reveals why time cannot be saved or consumed, and why people who try to do so lose sight of what life is all about.

The German writer Michael Ende (1929–95) is better known for another fantasy, *The Neverending Story* (1979),[15] which was made into a successful Hollywood film with the same title (and two sequels). Ende despised the movie and even tried to stop it from being made, once he realized how it distorted his original story. (In fact, he went to the filming studio and was thrown out!) Whatever the merits of the films, they do not do justice to a remarkable children's novel that offers much to adults as well.

The Neverending Story begins with Bastian Balthasar Bux, a chubby boy perhaps ten or twelve years old who is bullied at school for his overactive imagination. One day Bastian stumbles into Coreander's Bookstore, where he discovers a strange-looking book with heavy leather binding, titled *The Neverending Story*. While the shopkeeper is distracted, he "borrows" the book and runs to the school attic, where he begins to read it and soon becomes engrossed.

In the book he learns that the Childlike Empress, the ruler of a country called Fantastica (it's called "Fantasia" in the film), has fallen ill in her Ivory Tower. Even more ominously, her land is being swallowed up by something that can only be described as *a Nothing*. Fantastica is not just being destroyed: it is literally being annihilated. The Empress summons Atreyu, a famous young warrior, and appoints him as her hero. He sets off on a quest that takes him to the giant turtle Morla the Aged One and the Swamps of

Sadness, where he is stung by Ygramul the Many. At the Southern Oracle he passes the ordeal of the Three Magic Gates and rides on the back of a white luckdragon named Falkor. He survives a man-eating werewolf and many other dangers, but can find no solution to the Nothing that continues to eat away at Fantastica. Despairing, he returns to the Empress—who thanks him for succeeding in his mission, for he has brought their savior back with him.

Up to this point, we have been enjoying a double narrative: reading in Ende's *The Neverending Story* about Bastian reading *The Neverending Story* that he found in the bookshop. Increasingly, Bastian has been drawn into the tale, and now he finds himself a part of it. It turns out that all of Atreyu's adventures have just been a device to bring Bastian to Fantastica. He himself is the savior that the Empress refers to, for the survival of Fantastica depends on him giving her a new name....

Why is it so important for Bastian to give her another name? We realize that the Nothing annihilating Fantastica is the disappearance of imagination in Bastian's—and our—world. The entire novel is an absorbing and thought-provoking demonstration of the importance of imagination, of what happens when the mind's imaginative abilities begin to fade because they are no longer valued by an increasingly utilitarian society. Giving the Empress a new name symbolizes Bastian's own participation in the creation of Fantastica, and as soon as he does so Bastian finds himself sucked into it, where he has many adventures while learning to cope with his new imaginative powers. His tale, however, is more than entertaining or clever. *The Neverending Story* is itself an example of the insightful point that

Ende is revealing about how our creativity relates to our world. Appropriately, the cover of the edition that we read, like the cover of the book that Bastian reads, shows an oval formed by two snakes, each swallowing the other's tail. Fantastica and our world: which contains the other? Or does each need the other?

Momo is a shorter and simpler book, but its critique of our obsession with saving time is razor sharp. The rest of this chapter offers a Buddhist perspective on it, with the help of the Japanese Zen master Eihei Dogen (1200–1253 A.D.), whose *Shobogenzo* includes some of the most profound Buddhist reflections on time. Dogen's obscure and epigrammatical reflections on human temporality— more precisely, on the delusive duality we usually experience between ourselves and the objective time we think we are in—are as incisive today as when he wrote them. *Momo* was published in 1973, and since then the temporal nightmare it depicts (predicts?) has become our everyday reality. Together, *Momo* and Dogen can help us understand how we "consume" time today and what a more healthy alternative would be like.

Saving Time

> *Life holds one great but commonplace mystery...time. Calendars and clocks exist to measure time, but that signifies little because we all know that an hour can seem an eternity or pass in a flash, according to how we spend it.*
> —Momo[16]

We first meet Momo in the ruins of an amphitheater, on the out-
skirts of an unnamed city in what seems to be modern Italy. She is a
homeless child who does not know her own age. Appearing from
nowhere, she moves into an underground chamber below the amphitheater, where she lives with the help of some people of modest
means who live nearby and like to visit her. Momo has a wonder-
fully calming influence and the marvelous gift of truly listening to
others. She helps end a feud between two old friends, Salvatore and
Nino, and even encourages a long-silent canary to start singing again.
She knows the value of each individual soul, so that even if someone feels that his life has been a total failure, after speaking to her
he realizes "that there was only one person like himself in the whole
world" (18–19). Homeless, ageless, appearing from nowhere with
one-pointed attention and selfless compassion: all of this suggests
comparisons with Zen enlightenment and the path of the bodhisattva.

The plot thickens around a secret army of men in gray suits who
are slowly taking over the city. As we discover later, they are not
human beings: they live on other people's time, by smoking cigars
rolled from their stolen "time-lilies." The gray men promise people
more time in the future if they will save it and deposit it in their
Time Bank now, but to do that their victims must speed up their
work, reduce their socializing, and destroy all their joy in life. The
mottoes of the gray men are "Time is precious—don't waste it!"
and "Time is money—save it!" (67). They not only deceive people,
they encourage what from a Buddhist perspective is a pernicious
delusion: the notion that time can be distinguished from the things
and events "in" it.

Figaro the barber is one of their first victims. When he is in a bad mood, feeling an utter failure and doubting the value of his existence, he succumbs to their spurious arguments and timesaving mathematics. One of the gray men recommends that he save time by eliminating all the activities that actually give meaning and quality to his life: caring for his elderly mother, visiting his friends, reading, and even daydreaming. Suddenly he becomes future oriented, with disastrous consequences. "The determination to save time now so as to be able to begin a new life sometime in the future had embedded itself in his soul like a poisoned arrow," yet the change in his lifestyle makes him increasingly restless and irritable. No matter how much time he saves, he never seems to have any extra, and his days grow shorter and shorter. "Many other inhabitants were similarly afflicted.... Admittedly, timesavers were better dressed...earned more money and had more to spend, but they looked tired, disgruntled, and sour, and there was an unfriendly light in their eyes.... It had ceased to matter that people should enjoy their work and take pride in it." In sum, "people never seemed to notice that, by saving time, they were losing something else. No one cared to admit that life was becoming ever poorer, bleaker and more monotonous...[for] time is life itself, and life resides in the human heart, and the more people saved, the less they had" (65, 66–67, 68).

Salvatore the bricklayer tells Momo that he often gets drunk because that is the only way he can stomach the stress of a speeded-up life and the shoddy workmanship that results. He complains that the "tenements we're putting up aren't places for people to live in— they're hen coops. It's enough to make you sick." He mourns the loss of job satisfaction but sees no answer except in daydreaming about the future. "It used to give me a kick when we built something worthwhile, but now…. Someday, when I've made enough money, I'm going to quit this job and do something different" (76–77). Ende's fantasy becomes all too similar to what has become everyday reality for most of us.

The innkeeper Nino and his wife Liliana are also victims of this accelerated and commercialized way of life. To increase his income in response to a rent increase, Nino ejects from his premises a group of poor, elderly men, including his wife's uncle. Liliana rejects such timesaving values—"If being heartless is the only way you can get somewhere in life, count me out"—and even Nino admits that the atmosphere in the inn "seems strange—cold somehow." So he decides to resist peer pressure and apologizes, briefly going back to the slower, simpler life where people are more highly valued than profits. Nevertheless, he too eventually succumbs. When Momo returns a year later she finds that his little tavern has become a self-service fast-food restaurant where all the customers eat in frantic haste, standing at counters because there are no chairs. Was Ende thinking of Ronald McDonald's empire, or Japan's fast-food noodle shops?

Ende also targets modern distractions and the excessive consumerism that results in family breakdown and the increasing inability of children to use their imaginations. After the gray men start changing society, most of the new children who come to the amphitheater do not know how to play. They turn up with the kinds of toys you cannot really play with: remote controlled tanks and other expensive novelties such as Momo's friends have never owned. Such toys leave nothing to the imagination and the children end up mesmerized but bored. Family life deteriorates quickly. One little girl goes to the cinema every day because the ticket costs her parents less than a baby-sitter. Another boy has eleven books on tape because his mother is out all day and his father is too tired to tell him stories anymore. One child argues that "the grown-ups dish out money to get rid of us," and they all sadly admit to feeling abandoned (73).

The gray men tempt Momo with Lola the Living Doll, a talking Barbie-type toy with a never-ending wardrobe of clothes, accessories, and friends to accumulate. It is the perfect way to teach children the important economic lesson that "there's always something left to wish for." According to the gray man who pushes Lola on Momo, "All that matters in life is to climb the ladder of success, amount to something, own things. When a person climbs higher than the rest, amounts to more, owns more things, everything else comes automatically: friendship, love, respect, et cetera" (87).

Because of the importance of imagination in childhood, and a child's ability to live so much in the present, the gray men believe that children present a greater threat to their work than anyone or anything else, being "natural enemies. But for them, mankind would have been completely in our power long ago. Adults are far easier to turn into timesavers." They persuade adults to legislate against the free time and daydreaming enjoyed by children, arguing that children are "the raw material of the future," the experts and technicians of tomorrow who must be trained today (106–7, 167).

In compulsory, prisonlike "child depots" (our day-care centers, kindergartens, and schools?) children are allowed only educational games. So "they forgot how to be happy, how to take pleasure in little things, and, last but not least, how to dream." As the conditioning took effect "the children began to look like time-savers in miniature. Sullen, bored and resentful, they did as they were told" (168). When Momo meets three old playmates a year later she finds them in gray uniforms, their faces stiff and lifeless, on their way to class to learn games that are no fun but useful for the future. As in *The Neverending Story,* Ende questions modern utilitarianism: that everything we do is a preparation for something else more important.

When an agent fails to bribe Momo, the men in gray decide to attack Momo's two best friends, Guido Guide the storyteller (who is removed by turning him into a media celebrity) and Beppo Roadsweeper (who is put in a mental hospital). Guido's stories become so popular they make him rich and famous, but also keep him so busy that finally all his time is controlled by secretaries who bustle him about.

As a road sweeper Beppo has been deliberately slow, even Zen-like in his total attention to the present moment. In order to sweep all day long he had learned that it doesn't work to hurry: "You must only concentrate on the next step, the next breath, the next stroke of the broom, and the next, and the next. Nothing else…. That way you enjoy your work, which is important, because then you make a good job of it. And that's how it ought to be" (36). In traditional Japan he might have been regarded as a Buddhist master, but in the new, efficient, timesaving world he is believed to be "not quite right

in the head because he takes all the time he needs to answer questions, being determined never to say anything untrue" (35). When
Beppo tries to escape from his hospital, a gray man appears, lies to
him that Momo has been kidnapped, and releases him only after
Beppo agrees to ransom her with one hundred thousand hours of
hard—and hurried—work.

In the meantime Momo has been led by the tortoise Cassiopeia
to the magical residence of Professor Secundus Minutus Hora, who
lives in Nowhere House on Never Lane, where "all the time in the
world comes from." He is the custodian of time but has no personal
power to stop the time thieves because "What people do with their
own time is their own business" (143). However, he is a sworn enemy of the gray men and the only one they fear more than Momo.

Professor Hora teaches her the secret of time by showing her its
source: the hour-lilies. Momo has a mystical experience watching
the lilies blossom and fade as time's pendulum swings back and forth.
She begins to hear music and then "the sun and moon and planets and
stars were telling her their own, true names, and their names signi-
fied what they did and how they all combined to make each hour-lily
flower and fade in turn." She realizes with awe that "the entire universe was focused upon her like a single face of unimaginable size,
looking at her and talking to her." The professor tells Momo that
she has been in the depths of her own heart, watching her own time,
for "There's a place like the one you visited in every living soul, but
only those who let me take them there can reach it, nor can it be seen
with ordinary eyes" (147, 148). *Momo* contains no allusions to
Buddhism, yet despite its own distinctive symbolism this incident

seems to reflect a Buddhist-like sensibility in its emphasis on realizing the true nature of the universe by going deep inside ourselves.

Then Momo falls asleep for a year and a day. When she awakens all her friends are gone and life has changed into a nightmare of time-saving efficiency.

Professor Hora devises a plan to help her fight against the time thieves. He can stop time, but only for one hour, by giving her a special time-flower. During that period she must find the gray men's secret hoard of frozen time-lilies and release every stolen minute. If she does not succeed, the gray men will poison the air around Nowhere House with their cigar smoke and make everyone ill with a fatal disease called "deadly tedium." People will become increasingly bored until "you don't feel anything any more…. Joy and sorrow, anger and excitement are things of the past. You forget how to laugh and cry—you're cold inside and incapable of loving anything or anybody…. You bustle around with a blank, gray face, just like the men in gray themselves—indeed you've joined their ranks" (215).

We are not surprised, however, that Momo succeeds. The lily flowers return to their true home in human hearts, whereupon people suddenly find that they have plenty of time to spare. "Children played in the middle of the street, getting in the way of cars whose drivers not only watched and waited, smiling broadly, but sometimes got out and joined in their games. People stood around chatting with the friendliness of those who take a genuine interest in their neighbours' welfare" (235).

Everyone's sense of time returns to normal—in Momo, at least. But have the gray men taken over our own world? Ende wrote this fable before he visited Tokyo, where he must have observed the hordes of gray-suited "salarymen" infected with deadly tedium.[17] As this suggests, the gray men are not a Western or a Japanese problem but a modern problem. What does Buddhism have to say about the source of this problem?

Objectifying Time

> *"[My disciples] do not repent of the past, nor do they brood over the future. They live in the present. Therefore they are radiant. By brooding over the future and repenting the past, fools dry up like green reeds cut down."*
>
> —Buddha

Mahayana Buddhist teachings help us understand our problem with time by tracing it back to the basic dualism that we experience between things (including ourselves) and the time they are "in." This dualism is a fundamental delusion that contributes greatly to our *dukkha*, or unhappiness. Fortunately for us, this perceived split between things and their time is not something real or objective but rather is mentally constructed—which means it can be deconstructed.

The problem is not simply that everything dear to us (including ourselves) will pass away, nor is the solution simply to accept that impermanence. Such a response still presupposes the delusive duality between things and time. As realized by Nagarjuna, the great second-century Indian Buddhist philosopher, if there is no permanence then there can be no impermanence either, because the meaning of each is dependent upon the other: "All things are impermanent, which means there is neither permanence nor impermanence."[18] Unless there is something permanent to provide a fixed standard for reference, there is no way to be aware of impermanence as impermanence. Without nouns (things) there are no referents for verbs (past, present, and future tenses). When there are no things that have an existence *in* time, then it makes no sense to describe something as being young or old. "So the young man does not grow old nor does the old man grow old."[19]

If there are no things that exist in time, however, how is it that you are able to read this book? Isn't it because you bought it (or borrowed it) last week? Nagarjuna's argument is too abstract to connect easily with our everyday experience. Here Dogen's more concrete images can be more helpful. He uses them to deconstruct the dualism between things and time, by reducing each to the other.

From the one side, Dogen demonstrates that *objects are time,* because they have no existence outside of time. Objects are necessarily temporal, in which case they are really not objects according to our usual understanding, which unreflectively assumes them to have an existence apart from the time they are "in." If an object is something that is always temporal, then things like apples and cups cannot be objects as usually understood, because their impermanent "being" is actually a *process* (although perhaps a very slow one, as in the case of a cup that might endure for many years before being broken).

Dogen also makes the same point from the other side, by demonstrating that *time is objects.* Time for us is inseparable from things because our awareness of it depends on the way things change (for example, the way the second hand of a clock circles around in a clockwise direction). As Einstein discovered, time does not exist in and of itself. It is not an objectively existing "container" of self-existent things; rather, it manifests itself *as* the temporal processes we call objects—in which case time too must be different from how it is usually understood. "The time we call spring blossoms directly as an existence called flowers. The flowers, in turn, express the time called spring. This is not existence within time; existence itself is time."[20]

In his *Shobogenzo,* Dogen combines subject and predicate in the Japanese neologism *uji,* which is usually rendered into English as "being-time."

"Being-time" here means that time itself is being...and all being is time....

Time is not separate from you, and as you are present, time does not go away....

Do not think that time merely flies away. Do not see flying away as the only function of time. If time merely flies away, you would be separated from time. The reason you do not clearly understand being-time is that you think of time as only passing.... People only see time's coming and going, and do not thoroughly understand that time-being abides in each moment....

Being-time has the quality of flowing.... Because flowing is a quality of time, moments of past and present do not overlap or line up side by side.... Do not think flowing is like wind and rain moving from east to west.

The entire world is not unchangeable, is not immovable. It flows. Flowing
is like spring. Spring with all its numerous aspects is called flowing. When
spring flows there is nothing outside of spring.[21]

When time flows, there is nothing—no *thing*—outside of it. To
treat time as a commodity that can be saved, then, is to be caught
in a delusion. We hurry up in order to gain the time to slow down.
This is just the trap that *Momo*'s gray-suited time thieves encourage people to fall into. The commodifying attitude that tries to save
time cannot help but carry over into the rest of our lives. Understanding time as a resource, to be used like any other resource, means
we lose the ability to *be* what Dogen calls being-time. Since we are
so habituated to hurrying, it has become difficult for us to slow
down, even in situations when hurrying is inappropriate. How many
of us now take our laptops and cell phones with us when we go on
vacation?

The relativity of objects and time means that objective time—
time as a self-existing container for things—is a delusion.
Paradoxically, *if there is only time, there is no time.* I become "being-time" when I no longer situate my activities within a clock-time
understood as a container external to me. Then, in place of the present as a thin, ever-moving line between the immensities of past and
future, I live in (or *as*) the "eternal now" whenever I *become* what
I am doing.

This is not easy to understand, but it is the heart of the issue. If
every thing already *is* time—if, for example, the "being" of a flower
is its gesture of blossoming—then we are freed from the delusion

that time is something external to the flower, a container outside the flower. The same is true for us. If time is what I already am— if, for example, my "being" when I am dancing *is* my dancing— then that dancing-time (one form of my "being-time") is not something objective and outside me that I am within. That is because me and "my" time are nondual.

In other words, the Buddhist solution to this aspect of our suffering involves realizing that I am not *in* time because I *am* time. What I do and what happens to me are not events that occur in time; they are the forms that my being-time takes. If I *am* time, though, I cannot be trapped *by* time. Paradoxically, then, to be time is to be free from time. Momo is free because she lives in such a timeless world. It is not that she *has* time for her friends. Rather, her way of listening to them is loving and nourishing because her being-time is open to their being-time. Figaro the barber tries to save something that cannot be saved because time is not something we can ever *have*. We can only *be* it.

We rarely realize that, however. In individualistic modern cultures, my time is *mine*. I cherish and guard it from encroachment. I may need to sell a certain amount of it for money every week, but the rest belongs to me. I can spend it however I like; it is part of my disposable income. Today we take this for granted, and base all our business and recreational planning on this premise. Yet premodern cultures show us that such an individualistic attitude is not natural or inevitable. Unfortunately, this possessive attitude often encourages an indifference to civic concern and community issues, because we begrudge spending our time on them. Without collaborative participation, however, our burgeoning social and ecological problems are unlikely to be resolved. It is no coincidence that Momo, who does not begrudge her own time, is the one who saves the day.

That Nagarjuna and Dogen both emphasize the same problematical duality with time reminds us that our basic problem with it is neither modern nor Western. Contemporary time compression merely aggravates the delusive split between time and the things "in" it. Does this mean that objectifying time is a basic tendency of the human condition? Is this habit common to all cultures? Apparently not. In contrast to modern societies, some premodern tribal ones lack awareness of objective time as an abstract reference point outside the events that happen *within* it. The anthropologist E.E. Evans-Pritchard concludes his classic study on the Nuer of central Africa somewhat wistfully: "I do not think that they ever experience the same feeling of fighting against time or having to coordinate activities with an abstract passage of time, because their points of reference are mainly the activities themselves, which are generally of a leisurely character. Events follow in a logical order, but they are not controlled by an abstract system, there being no autonomous points of reference to which activities have to conform with precision."[22]

What exaggerates the duality today are modern technologies and forms of social organization that enable us to quantify time and coordinate our schedules more precisely. Commodification was made possible, and perhaps inevitable, by the clock. As clock-time became central to social organization, life became "centered around the emptying out of time (and space) and the development of an abstract, divisible and universally measurable calculation of time."[23] The collective objectification of clock-time means that now, insofar as we are social beings, we must live according to this universal standard. The complexities of our social interactions require such a mechanism for their coordination, even though such a lifeless way of patterning time alienates us from natural temporal rhythms, including those of our own body. Nevertheless, most of the time we have no choice but to pay attention to the clock. In order to get to work (or class) by 9:00 A.M., we have to catch the 8:16 bus.

In other words, time today does function as an objective container for us, like it or not, for that is the way it has been socially constructed, and understanding that construction is a necessary part of our socialization. Children must internalize that collective construction, for it is needed to coordinate our activities. But to live *only* according to that collective construct is to "bind ourselves without a rope," to use the Zen metaphor for self-imposed restriction. With clock-time, time is objectified and regulates the activity from outside. With Dogen's being-time, in contrast, the temporality of an activity becomes integral to the activity itself. We can sometimes notice this difference in, for example, the way music is played. Often the notes march along precisely following the time signature, but sometimes we become so absorbed in those notes that we do not notice the time signature at all because the music nondually embodies its own time.

The musical example is a good one because it reminds us that the solution is not always to slow down. Some music sounds better played fast. Many sports would not be much fun if you could not run. The point is to find the pace that is appropriate for the activity—or, stated less dualistically, to let events generate their own temporality. Most of us know better than to make love watching the clock. Can we learn to love the whole world like that, in all our activities? Does Momo show us the way? Her way of playing with children and being with friends is not constricted by time pressures. Her being-time naturally flows from one activity to the other. But it is easier to do that when you don't have a job, or rent to pay, or need to get the kids to school on time.

The Lack of Time

If time commodification and consumption are such a problem, why have we come to distinguish so sharply between absolute clock-time and the events that happen "in" it? According to Anthony Aveni, an anthropologist who studies different time systems, the common drive behind human temporal schemas is a quest for order, which is necessary to secure the cosmos and the self that inhabits it. "Temporally speaking, we desire the capacity to anticipate where things are going, to relieve our anxiety by peeking around nature's corner as far as it will follow."[24]

Deeper than that desire for order, however, is what Damian Thompson in *The End of Time* describes as our "deep-seated human urge to escape from time which, in the earliest societies, was usually met by dreams of a return to a golden past."[25] Christian expectations of an imminent Apocalypse changed that, by situating us toward the end rather than the beginning of time. We began to look forward to a golden future instead, although not one to be enjoyed in this world. Then, in a crucial step toward modernity, the Italian hermit Joachim of Fiore (1135–1202) conceived of a coming golden age not outside of this world (in heaven) but *within* it. It was this shift in perspective that eventually developed into our modern preoccupation with progress.

Perhaps the difference between a golden past and a golden future is less important than their common inclination to avoid something about the now. What is it about the *now* that makes us uncomfortable? A poignant passage in *Momo* touches on this issue. During their conversation Momo asks Professor Hora if he is Death, and he replies: "If people knew the nature of death... they'd cease to be afraid of it. And if they ceased to be afraid of it, no one could rob them of their time any more" (144). We try to save time because there is something about our temporality that terrifies us. Thompson sums up his study of apocalyptic time by concluding that the human understanding of time is always distorted by death: "The belief that mankind has reached the crucial moment in its history reflects an unwillingness to come to terms with the transience of human life and achievements. Our urge to celebrate the passing of time fails to conceal an even deeper urge to escape from it."[26]

In contrast, Buddhism begins with the historical Buddha's willingness to come to terms with the transience of human life and achievements. According to the traditional myth, it was Shakyamuni's encounter with an old man, an ill man, a corpse, and finally a renouncer that motivated his spiritual quest. Our terror and denial of death will be the focus of Chapter 5. Given Buddhism's emphasis on *anatta* "no-self", however, an explanation of time compression and commodification that focuses solely on death-denial and symbolic immortality may be incomplete. The no-self teaching suggests that something else more immediate is also bothering us.

Time as an objective container, necessary to coordinate our activities, is not the only aspect of our experience that has been constructed. *Anatta* implies something more fundamental: that even my sense of being an individual self is a conditioned mental construct. There is some sense of this constructedness in our awareness of being ungrounded, but that is an uncomfortable feeling which we tend to repress. As Freud realized, however, repression does not usually work, for what has been repressed finds a way to return to consciousness, in this case as a sense of lack: the feeling that "something is wrong with me." We all experience this lack yet understand it in different ways ("I'm not rich enough, famous enough, loved enough…"), according to the kind of person we are and the kind of culture we have been socialized into.

Another way to describe it is that we do not feel real enough—which is quite true: the sense of self, being a mental construction, is not real at all. Our response is to try to become more real, more grounded, which is where religion traditionally comes in. Many religions offer a simple, reassuring solution: what is wrong with us is sin (or something like that), but if we go to church on Sunday, or pray five times a day, etc., then we will be saved (that is, we will feel more real when we are with God in heaven). Such religious solutions are less attractive in a secular and more individualistic society, where many people have become skeptical about God and not as worried about sin. In the modern world we still feel unreal and ungrounded, yet becoming real now depends more on our own personal efforts, which require us to use our time efficiently.

For Buddhism, then, the sense of self is better understood not as a thing but as an ongoing *process* that seeks perpetually, although unsuccessfully, to ground and secure itself by becoming more real. Moreover, since our modern sense of self is more individualized, it tends to be all the more unsatisfied with itself. If I am dissatisfied, the reason must be that I have not *attained my goals*! Since the goals I do accomplish bring no relief from my sense of lack, I need ever more ambitious projects, which means ever greater time compression. Of course, not everyone is motivated in this fashion, but modern individualism encourages this way of understanding our sense of lack.

In psychological terms, the pressure we feel to accomplish something is an internalization of the intentions we project outward into the world. The psychoanalyst Neil Altman noticed his own compulsion to accomplish something during his years as a Peace Corps volunteer in southern India. Raised in an individualistic culture emphasizing achievement more than affiliation, Altman, like most of us, had been trained to use his time efficiently: "It took a year for me to shed my American, culturally based feeling that I had to make something happen.... Being an American, and a relatively obsessional American, my first strategy was to find security through getting something done, through feeling worthwhile accomplishing something. My time was something that had to be filled up with progress toward that goal."[27]

Time must be used efficiently to make progress toward our goals. When we are obsessed by that attitude, however, we lose Momo's and Dogen's being-time. Since we can never fill up our sense of lack in this way, we can never "have" enough time. But how else can we deal with our sense of lack? According to Buddhism, anatta—our lack of a substantial self—opens up another possibility: awakening to my nonduality with the world, realizing that I am not other than my world. I am not "in" the world, I am a manifestation of it. This is liberating because it frees me from the self-preoccupation of always trying to ground myself. Once I have realized this by letting go of my self, there is nothing that needs to be made real, and there is no need to use my time efficiently to do so.

That does not mean we can ignore collective clock-time as a social construction, but we are no longer trapped within it. We free ourselves insofar as our lives become more playful. Playing is what we are doing when we do not need to gain something from a situation. When we do not devalue the here and now in order to extract something from it for the future, then, like Momo's old friends, we may discover that there is the time—the being-time—to smell the flowers as we do our work with loving care.

> People stood around chatting with the friendliness of those who take a genuine interest in their neighbors' welfare. Other people, on their way to work, had time to stop and admire the flowers in a window-box or feed the birds. Doctors, too, had time to devote themselves properly to their patients, and workers of all kinds did their jobs with pride and loving

care, now that they were no longer expected to turn out as much work as possible in the shortest possible time (235).

4

The Dharma of Nonviolence

Hayao Miyazaki's
Nausicaa of the Valley of the Winds
and *Princess Mononoke*

There is a black thing that infects your souls…. This is the curse of vengeance and hatred that rots the flesh and beckons death.
—Ashitaka in *Princess Mononoke*

Victory breeds hatred; the conquered dwell in sorrow. Those who have given up both victory and defeat are peaceful and live in harmony.
—Buddha in *The Dhammapada*

A S WELL AS TEACHING THE MIDDLE WAY, Shakyamuni Buddha was a peacemaker. Sometimes there were conflicts within the *sangha* (community of monastics) to resolve, but occasionally he intervened in more dangerous situations. In one incident, the peoples of Kapilavastu and Koliya were about to battle over water rights to the Rohini River, which meandered its way between them. Due to a drought the river did not have enough water to irrigate fields on both sides. Instead of working out a way to share what was available, the two clans had an argument that led to name-calling and then appeals to both kings, who took up arms to settle the issue.

Using his *siddhi* (supernatural powers), the Buddha observed from afar that the two cities were about to fight, and that this would lead to widespread misery. Bloodshed would stain red the waters of the Rohini. So, as the two kings approached the riverbanks, he appeared between them over the water, hovering cross-legged in midair, and spoke to the astonished combatants: "Is this water more valuable than all the blood about to be sacrificed because of it?" His words brought both sides to their senses, and the two kings agreed to settle their differences nonviolently.

But the Buddha was not always so successful. According to another story, Prince Vidudabha of Kosala harbored an intense hatred for the Shakyas (Shakyamuni's own clan) due to an old insult: when his father King Pasenadi had asked the Shakyas to send him a wife, they had contemptuously and secretly sent him a slave-girl, who gave birth to Vidudabha. When Vidudabha later discovered that his mother had been a slave, he was outraged. Upon ascending the throne he decided to destroy the Shakyas. In this case, too, the Buddha appeared before the bellicose king and his army as they marched to attack. Vidudabha looked over to where the Buddha was sitting, under a tree with too few branches to offer much protection against the afternoon sun, and commented that the tree did not provide enough shade to ward off the burning heat. The King invited the Buddha to refresh himself under the leafy banyan trees in his own land. The Buddha replied: "Taking a rest in the shade of one's many relations is what is cool and refreshing."

Vidudabha is said to have understood the Buddha's point—presumably, that the death of one's relatives and friends in war is a great loss, regardless of who "wins"—and returned home without attacking the Shakyas. His hatred was not appeased, however. Desire for revenge eventually led to his mounting a second and then a third campaign, but both times he again turned back when the Buddha reappeared. On the fourth attempt, the Buddha realized that the moment had come when the Shakyas could not avoid the consequences of their karma. King Vidudabha proceeded to massacre almost all of the Shakyas, and thus the Buddha's clan was destroyed.

Regardless of whether these incidents occurred historically in the manner recounted in the Pali sutras, we can still wonder about the meaning they have for us today. Maybe they warn us that we should not expect conciliatory words to save us from the consequences of our ill-doing—although, admittedly, annihilation of a whole clan seems an overreaction to an insult. Perhaps that, too, is a caution about how the world works: matters of great and even ultimate consequence for large groups of people can turn on perceived slights and nursed resentment. But cultivating ill will is not the Buddhist way:

"He abused me, he beat me, he defeated me, he robbed me."

For those who harbor such thoughts ill will [*vera*] will never cease.

"He abused me, he beat me, he defeated me, he robbed me."

For those who do not harbor such thoughts ill will will cease.

In this world hatred is never appeased by ill will

Ill will is always appeased by love [*avera*].

This is an ancient law.[28]

Do we find such nonviolence in modern fantasy? Peacemaking is not easy to dramatize effectively. Stories thrive on conflict, and violence usually enacts that struggle better than anything else. Resolution occurs when the bad guys are destroyed by the good ones, who live happily ever after. In Tolkien's *Lord of the Rings,* Frodo, Gandalf, and their companions deceive and finally defeat the evil forces of Sauron and Saruman. Ende's Momo outwits the gray men, who, deprived of their time-cigars, evaporate into the air. And in Pullman's *His Dark Materials* trilogy, Lyra and Will struggle against the life-denying control of "the Authority," as her parents fight and fall into the Abyss with Metatron, the evil Regent who wants to rule all the worlds. Our sense of justice is gratified when, in the climax, the bad guys are killed.

Yet we must not take these stories to be recommending physical force in our world. In Buddhist terms, we might say that in these fantasies violence operates as a metaphor for the struggle that occurs within us when we try to transform the three poisons of greed, ill will, and delusion (represented by the bad guys) into the three virtues of generosity, loving-kindness, and wisdom (embodied in the good guys).

But if myths work by depicting moral and spiritual conflict as physical violence, what about a fantasy that tries to challenge "the myth of redemptive violence," the widespread belief that aggression is an acceptable and effective way to resolve differences? How then is peacemaking—the struggle against violence—to be depicted symbolically and in a convincing way?

One of the last places we might expect such a nonviolent myth is in animated film, which usually depends on physical conflict for its visual appeal. Japanese *anime*, in particular, are known for their graphic depiction of sexuality and violence. And yet it is in two of the most acclaimed films of Japan's most celebrated animator that we find thoughtful and moving depictions of a Buddhist-like alternative to violence.

Hayao Miyazaki

Japan, in the eyes of most Western Buddhists, is the land of Zen and its unique aesthetic, including haiku, the tea ceremony, and brush painting. Today a new art deserves to be added to that list: the *anime* of Hayao Miyazaki, whose exceptionally beautiful, sometimes haunting films are still too little known in the West. Although they contain few explicit religious references, Buddhist themes and perspectives play a major role in what we believe to be his best films.

Hayao Miyazaki (b. 1941) is the most respected filmmaker in contemporary Japan, and his success is well deserved. His Studio Ghibli is responsible for a series of classic films that have raised feature-length animation from mass entertainment to the highest standard of artistic excellence, and done so without sacrificing its popular appeal. In Japan his *anime* are much more popular than imported Disney films at cinema box offices. For most *manga* (Japanese comic book) and *anime* fans, Miyazaki is practically a god. The release of a new Miyazaki film has become an eagerly awaited cultural event.

But what place do his animated films have in a book on Buddhist themes in modern fantasy? Miyazaki has said that he makes his films only to entertain,[29] yet his best *anime* do much more than that. In contrast to the usual conventions of that genre, his visual fantasies give us convincing models of how to live in a complicated and often confusing world—and they are important models, since the extraordinary commercial success of his films in Japan means they provide a very viable alternative to the "lowest common denominator" that marketplace commodification tends to encourage. He has often focused on the challenges for girls growing up in contemporary Japan, depicting young female protagonists in ways that give adolescents confidence about themselves, empowering them in a culture that remains very patriarchal. This is an important theme in many of his best films: for example, *My Neighbor Totoro* (1988), *Kiki's Delivery Service* (1989), and more recently *Spirited Away* (2001)—perhaps the most gorgeous animated film of all time—which won an Academy Award for best animated feature.

My Neighbor Totoro remains the favorite of many Miyazaki fans. We do not know a more endearing film for young children, but there is much to charm grownups as well. In her fine book on Miyazaki's œuvre, the *anime* critic Helen McCarthy gives it the highest praise: "*My Neighbor Totoro* is both my favorite Miyazaki work and my favorite film. Its apparent simplicity masks a depth of wisdom and grace found in few works for any medium. It is accessible to even the youngest child, yet it respects the intelligence of the most literate and cultivated adult."[29]

Set in rural Japan sometime after World War II, *My Neighbor Totoro* tells the story of two little girls who move with their father into a large countryside house. While their mother lies ill in a nearby hospital and their father busies himself with his work, Mei and her big sister Satsuki explore the enchanted world around them. They literally bump into a cuddly animal-spirit called Totoro, ascend on spinning tops above a giant camphor tree, and help magic seeds to sprout. When Mei becomes lost trying to visit her mother, Totoro summons his friend the Cat-Bus, who takes Satsuki on a wild ride to find her sister, who sits forlornly by six statues of Jizo (the Japanese bodhisattva associated most closely with children, a rare allusion to Buddhism). After a brief visit to their mother's clinic, they return home in the Cat-Bus, and as the closing credits roll we see a series of stills showing their happy future, when their mother comes home to rejoin them. This bald summary cannot capture the wisdom and grace that McCarthy refers to, but Miyazaki's unsentimental affection and insight into the lives of children are palpable throughout.

Another favorite is *Kiki's Delivery Service*, whose teenage heroine sets out to find her own way in life. In addition to her cheerful enthusiasm, she has only one skill to offer the world: being the child of a witch, she can fly. But it is time for Kiki to leave her countryside home and make a new life for herself in the big city, accompanied only by her faithful (and talkative) black cat, Jiji. She finds a job delivering cakes for a bakery and meets Ursula, a young artist living in a forest cabin, who encourages her when she loses confidence. Supporting herself and making new friends turn out to be challenging, but in the end Kiki begins to spread her own wings. We find this film a charming fable delicately addressing the issues that concern most young people as they make the often difficult transition to independence. Viewers learn with Kiki what it means to become an adult.

There are many other Miyazaki *anime* that we love: in fact, almost all of them. Here, however, our concern is the Buddhist dimension of his films, which is quite striking despite the fact that overtly religious images and references are not usually significant in Miyazaki's work, in large part because his deepest spiritual concerns are assimilated into the plots as central themes. One of the reasons this works so well is because the spiritual is usually understood as immanent, as integrated into the natural world, rather than residing in a monotheistic being or transcendental force. This chapter explores Miyazaki's "Dharma" by discussing *Nausicaa of the Valley of the Winds* (1984) and *Princess Mononoke* (1997). Our focus is on what these insightful *anime* say—or rather, show—about the problem of evil and violence and how to respond to it.

Revenge versus Compassion

Nausicaa tells the tale of another teenage girl, who is called upon to do much more than merely grow up. Although quite complicated, the plot is a simplified version of a *manga* comic book series that Miyazaki wrote and illustrated. The story takes place in a post-apocalyptic future after war and ecological disaster have destroyed technological civilization and poisoned much of the natural world. Nausicaa is the inquisitive and fearless daughter of King Jhil, who rules over the Valley of the Winds. At the beginning we see Nausicaa flying on her jet-powered glider, exploring the poisoned forest (while protected by a mask) and then saving her mentor Yupa when he is chased by an angry Ohmu, which looks something like a gigantic beetle.

Soon after they return to the Valley of the Winds, a hijacked Tolmekian battleship crashes into the mountains surrounding the valley. In the wreckage Nausicaa finds the dying Princess Lastelle of Pejitei, who begs her to destroy the airship's cargo. But a monstrous, pulsating "God Warrior" has survived, and soon Tolmekian warships invade the Valley to recover the creature and force its people to help them destroy the poisoned forest, which threatens to infect everything else. In the attack King Jhil is killed and Nausicaa reacts explosively, killing several soldiers before Yupa is able to calm her. Later she has recovered enough to pacify her outraged kinfolk when they hear about King Jhil's death: "Please listen to me. I don't want any more death.... Let's obey these people." This is a striking moment in the film: since when do *anime* heroes urge surrender? In place of the usual justified rage against the baddies, this acknowledges the insight that revenge only perpetuates the cycle of violence that the Buddha identified millennia ago.

Kushana, princess of the invading Tolmekians, decides to visit home. She takes Nausicaa and others with her as hostages, but their fleet is attacked by a lone Pejitean fighter that destroys several of their aircraft. When Nausicaa tries to stop the attack by interposing herself—another striking example of nonviolent selflessness—the Pejitean pilot hesitates, and his own plane is hit by fire. After some adventures Nausicaa and the pilot end up in a huge cavernous area hidden beneath the poisoned world below, where to their surprise they find that the air and water are pure. Nausicaa has an epiphany as she realizes that the forest is not the ecological problem but the solution: it has been slowly purifying itself of the toxic chemicals created by humans.

It turns out that the Pejitean pilot, Asbel, is none other than Lastelle's twin brother, attacking the Tolmekian fleet for revenge. The next morning they fly back to the city of the Pejiteans and discover to their horror that it has been destroyed by the Tolmekians and a swarm of Ohmu. In response, the surviving Pejiteans plan to incite the Ohmu to attack Nausicaa's Valley of the Winds and destroy the Tolmekians still there. Appalled, Nausicaa manages to escape with the help of some sympathetic Tolmekian women. Speeding home on her glider, she sees a baby Ohmu being tortured by Pejitean soldiers in order to enrage and lure the massed Ohmu. Nausicaa, however, manages to save the little Ohmu and forces the Pejitean soldiers to drop them both in front of the charging Ohmu swarm. Although their stampede tramples her, the Ohmu are mollified and stop at the edge of the Valley. As their glowing tentacles lift her up, Nausicaa comes back to life. The baby Ohmu revives, Nausicaa is saved, and her people and the Tolmekians stop fighting each other.

Although *Nausicaa of the Valley of the Winds* contains plenty of violence, what stands out most is the heroine's revulsion against it, and her willingness to put herself in danger to stop the killing. In Buddhist terms, she too becomes a bodhisattva, selflessly committed to doing whatever she can to help all those tragically caught in a reinforcing cycle of hatred and revenge.

Thirteen years later, in 1997, Miyazaki's Studio Ghibli released *Princess Mononoke,* which quickly broke all records as Japan's most successful film ever. Within five months it had been viewed by 12 million people, approximately one-tenth of the population of Japan; the video release sold 2 million copies within three weeks. It remains Miyazaki's most acclaimed work, combining breathtaking animation with psychological subtlety.

Princess Mononoke is set in medieval Japan, where ecological destruction is beginning as people learn to forge iron by mining and logging the primeval forest. Despite the title, we experience the story through the eyes of Ashitaka, a young man who is forced to kill a terrible monster, a boar god writhing with bloodworms, when it attacks his village. It turns out that the boar had been driven mad by a mysterious lump of iron embedded in its flesh. In dispatching the creature, Ashitaka is himself injured in the arm, a cursed infection that, he is told, will spread and eventually kill him. Forced to leave the village, he fights some cruel samurai and discovers that his curse also gives him extraordinary fighting ability.

After a brief visit to another village, where he meets the itinerant priest Jiko, Ashitaka ends up in the middle of a ferocious struggle between a human settlement called Irontown and forest creatures who are resisting the destruction of their natural world. Both sides are led by women. The leader of Irontown is Lady Eboshi, who is an especially interesting and complex character: a feminist who provides a safe home for prostitutes and lepers, but who also does not mind ravaging the earth to make iron and guns. On the other side is San (Princess Mononoke), raised by the wolf god Moro. She wants to defend the forest by killing Eboshi. San attacks Irontown and ends up in single combat with Eboshi—a duel stopped by Ashitaka, who uses his new powers to knock them both unconscious and carry San back into the forest. In the process he is shot in the back, but that wound is healed by the god of the forest, Shishigami, who does not, however, lift the curse that still condemns him. Like Nausicaa, Ashitaka becomes a bodhisattva, selflessly doing whatever he can to stop the violence between Irontown and the creatures of the forest.

Outside, the boar gods confer with the wolf gods on what to do about the humans. Eboshi is ready for a confrontation, but she does not realize that a double-cross has been planned. While the men of Irontown are out fighting an epic battle with the beasts, another samurai warlord attacks their home. There are huge losses on all sides, but meanwhile something even more ominous is going on. Jiko, it turns out, is an agent of the emperor, who craves the head of the god of the forest because of a legend that it can confer immortality. Eboshi, who owes Jiko a favor, uses one of her guns to shoot Shishigami, and all hell breaks loose.

Such Gods do not die easily. Out of his neck flows a translucent fluid that kills everything it touches. It spreads quickly over the mountains and even into Irontown, whose inhabitants escape just in time. After struggling with Jiko, however, Ashitaka and San manage to restore the head to the God, who in the climax nevertheless collapses into the lake below Irontown. Despite the horrible devastation of this cataclysm and all the fighting, some people and forest creatures have survived. At the end, Eboshi vows to rebuild Irontown. San cannot forgive the humans for the awful things they have done, but she has come to love Ashitaka. Ashitaka, whose infected arm is now healing, will help Irontown rebuild, and spend time with San in the forest when he can.

Good versus Evil

Needless to say, these simplified plot summaries cannot do justice to either *Nausicaa* or *Mononoke*, which on a full-sized cinema screen are stunningly beautiful as well as emotionally gripping. What deserves to be emphasized is that these two *anime* should be appreciated in relation to each other, because the parallels between them are quite extraordinary. Both gain a mythic perspective on the present by being set in historically distant times—one in the distant future, the other in the distant past. Miyazaki has said that the setting for *Nausicaa* was inspired by the mercury poisoning of Minamata Bay by a chemical factory in the 1950s, "which sent shivers up my spine." Both films present imaginative, detailed animal worlds where "the right of every living thing to cling to life is unquestioned. Miyazaki said that *Nausicaa* itself 'was inspired by a kind of animism,'"[30] something obviously true for *Mononoke* also. In contemporary terms, Miyazaki would have to be considered a deep ecologist, for his obvious belief that the natural world does not exist only for humans to exploit it; rather, the flourishing of all the earth's creatures has its own intrinsic value, independent of their usefulness for us. The natural-world context for these two films offers an interesting contrast to some of his other films, which gain much of their attraction from how well they depict ordinary life today in urban Japan.

Traditional religion plays no significant role in either film, despite the presence of two oracles, both old women. Lady Hii banishes Ashitaka from his home village at the beginning of *Mononoke*; Nausicaa's grandmother is a seer who tells her the prophecy of the valley's savior and at the end of the film declares that Nausicaa has fulfilled it. Both films are striking, from a Western perspective at least, in that the relationships between humans and gods, and between humans and nature, are really the same: the spiritual and the natural are nondual. The natural world is not something that has been created by a transcendental God, for humans to use as they like. Shishigami the god of the forest does not rule the forest, he embodies the forest. Nature itself is numinous and salvation is to be found in realizing our oneness with it.

Given the double-sided threat in both films—the human threat to the natural world, and poisoned nature's threat to human society—there is an obvious ecological focus, but that axis between humans and nature is supplemented by another one, at least as important, between hatred/violence and selfless compassion. Both storylines are motivated by revenge, which rationalizes the violence of one group against another. Both plots focus on challenging the myth of redemptive violence, and powerfully depict a nonviolent alternative that highlights the healing power of compassion.

How do they subvert the cycle of hatred reinforcing more hatred? The films avoid any simple duality between good (us) and evil
(them)—a good group defending itself against the evil threat of an
outside group—by counterposing a third element. In place of the
usual contrast, each shows us three clans, presented against the
backdrop of a threatened and threatening nature. In each case one
of those societies is a peace-loving backwater, home to the protag-
onist (Nausicaa or Ashitaka), who takes it upon her- or himself to
mediate and resolve wars both with the natural world and between
the other human clans. In attempting to stop the fighting, Nausicaa
and Ashitaka are both badly wounded, and they are both healed by
the spiritual power of nature.

Again, neither film contains any explicit or implicit reference to
Buddhism, but each hero responds to the violent struggles of others
by developing into a bodhisattva. In the early sutras of the Pali
Canon, that term describes only the previous lifetimes of Shakyamuni,
the historical Buddha. In later Mahayana Buddhism, however, a
bodhisattva is any Buddha-in-training whose advanced spiritual
practice involves selfless and wholehearted commitment to "saving" all beings, especially (but not only) by helping them awaken
to their inherent buddha-nature. As Nausicaa and Ashitaka exemplify, this often involves self-sacrifice, followed by a resurrection
that symbolizes transformation into a higher stage of egoless wisdom
and purity of spirit.

Nausicaa is almost too perfect as a noble-minded heroine, although she is not a one-dimensional cardboard figure. She flies
into a rage when the Tolmekians kill her father, King Jhil, but she

is restrained by her mentor, the wise swordsman Yupa, and she is able to let go of and then outgrow her desire for revenge. The main contrast of the film is between most people's resentment and her own compassion for all who are blindly caught up in their own violence. She constantly risks herself to stop the killing: to quiet her own people after her father's death; to defend a Tolmekian ship attacked by Asbel; to approach a Pejitean ship carrying a baby Ohmu; and in the climax, to stop the crazed attack of the swarming Ohmu. Her martyrdom and resurrection provide a pointed contrast with most other *anime* (and other action films) where the hero also risks himself—but always to kill the baddies.

It is significant that none of the clans or their leaders in *Nausicaa* is presented as "evil." Instead, the film challenges the usual simpleminded duality between good and evil. Each of the three different groups is trying to do the best it can, within its own worldview and limited understanding. The same is true for nature. The Ohmu, as representatives of the natural world, are depicted almost affectionately, despite the fear that they arouse in everyone except Nausicaa. Although their instinctive reactions to events are limited by lack of understanding, they are not patronized as subhuman monsters. In one of the most memorable scenes (with haunting music), Nausicaa has a vision in which she remembers an incident from her childhood, when she tried to protect a baby Ohmu. The Ohmu have magical healing powers, and throughout the film nature is depicted in a mysterious way that is to be respected rather than understood.

Change a few names, and almost all the above is also true for *Princess Mononoke*, which inspires us to think of it as practically a remake of the earlier film, as if Miyazaki were thinking through the same themes again, deepening and enriching them. Again, and even more clearly, the plot refuses to make any simple duality between good and evil. In this film too, most of the main characters do (or try to do) bad things, not because their nature is evil, but because they are complicated: sometimes because they are greedy or otherwise selfish, sometimes just because they are defending their own group. Another way to make the point is that they are so narrowly focused on what they are doing that they do not see the wider implications of their actions.

This is consistent with the emphasis that Buddhism places upon the three *roots* of evil, mentioned earlier as the three poisons: greed, ill will, and ignorance (or delusion). When they motivate our actions, evil tends to be the result. The ethical and spiritual challenge, then, is not physically destroying evil but transforming the roots of evil into their positive counterparts: generosity, loving-kindness, and wisdom. Both films show us plenty of greed, ill will, and delusion, while Nausicaa and Ashitaka demonstrate the alternatives.

In *Mononoke,* Ashitaka nonviolently attempts to mediate in the war between Lady Eboshi and San, the abandoned child who hates her own kind. Both women are depicted as attractive, even admirable figures, but they want to destroy each other. Eboshi does not mind cutting down the forest to make iron, "trying to build her idea of paradise—which makes her a twentieth-century person."[31] For her as for Kushana, the end justifies the means, yet she is also shown as a proto-feminist, compassionate to the lepers and former prostitutes in her care. Muddying the moral distinctions even more, Eboshi puts the lepers to work making guns, while the women forge iron. San identifies with the forest and the animals who dwell in it, and devotes herself to defending them against the encroachments of Irontown. Like Nausicaa interceding between Tolmekia and Pejitei, Ashitaka risks his own life trying to stop the violence between Eboshi and San, and later between their clans. As he interrupts their savage duel, he declares: "There is a black thing that infects your souls…. This is the curse of vengeance and hatred that rots the flesh and beckons death."

Like the giant Ohmu in *Nausicaa,* Shishigami the immanent god of the forest has a healing power that humans can participate in and benefit from. Here, too, *Mononoke* is more nuanced: the god of the forest grants life, but he also takes it away. Ashitaka has a spiritual epiphany when he first sees Shishigami, and another one when Shishigami appears to silently heal his gunshot wound; as with Nausicaa's own epiphany, these events occur in the depths of a sacred forest near a mystical pond surrounded by towering trees. The forest has a magical presence in both films, as it may have had for Shakyamuni, who was born under trees, meditated under trees, had his great awakening under trees, and passed away under trees. Yet the gods in *Mononoke* are not immortal. They can become diminished, even be killed, which is what is happening as humans begin to destroy their forest home.

Perhaps the most extraordinary plot parallel is that the climax of both films involves a double battle, in which animals attack while two human clans are fighting against each other. In both cases the animals have been tricked into attacking, enraged by human insensitivity and destructiveness. In both cases the greater intelligence of humans does not imply any moral superiority, since they use their cleverness in a mean-spirited way to instigate aggression and bloodshed. Nausicaa and Ashitaka try to stop the battles. Nausicaa is successful, Ashitaka is not.

Both finales involve resurrection: the miraculous healing of Nausicaa, trampled while stopping the Ohmu attack, and the restoration of Shishigami's head, which had been shot off by Lady Eboshi. Despite human deception and this act of deicide, however, humans are not stigmatized as evil, nor is nature romanticized. Nature can be stupid and wrathful, as we see in the suicidal rage of the boars, and especially at the conclusion of *Mononoke* when the life-force of the decapitated Shishigami becomes a death-force that destroys everything it touches—a powerful symbol for the destructiveness of nature when damaged by our collective greed and stupidity.

The problem of "collective ego" (or *"wego"*) refers to the fact that we tend to reinforce each other's greed, ill will, and delusion, thereby creating collective evil. The most disastrous example of such collective evil is not the group-sanctioned violence of war but human devastation of the earth, our mother as well as our home. From a Buddhist perspective, our most problematical individual delusion is *the self*—in other words, the sense of separation between oneself and others. Collectively, our most problematical delusion is the same: that is, the alienation between our group and another, between our nation and their nation, between our religion and their religion, between *Homo sapiens* and the rest of the biosphere—the last duality based on a collective stupidity regarding our interdependence with nature. In a way that may harbinger the future, the plots of Nausicaa and Mononoke are built upon the violent interaction between both dualities: war between tribal groups, along with struggle between humans and a violated natural world. As the consequences of various ecological crises interact and intensify, we can also expect increased tension between the human societies most affected by those developments.

At the end of *Mononoke*, Shishigami's head is restored, but nevertheless the forest god collapses and apparently dies. The more tragic vision of *Mononoke* means that "there can be no happy ending to the war between gods and mortals."[32] The death-force of the beheaded Shishigami can be said to represent the karmic consequences of our technological exploitation of the biosphere. If, however, his subsequent collapse symbolizes ecological breakdown, we should not expect to survive it as easily as Irontown does. *Nausicaa* has a happier ending: as the Ohmu retreat the different human clans are no longer fighting each other, and the fact that nature is slowly purifying itself of its poisons gives hope for the future. In *Mononoke*, however, there is no possibility of restoring ecological harmony between nature and humans. The film ends with an uneasy truce, everyone picking up the pieces. Too many have died in the ferocious battles; too much has been destroyed. The survivors of Irontown will rebuild under Eboshi's guidance. "Ashitaka and San meet again in the grasslands at the edge of the forest. He will never be able to go back to the innocent boy he was before the curse, but he has kept innocence and gentleness alive in his heart through all the deceit and disappointment he has faced. San will never trust humans and does not want to live in a human community, but she has learned that she loves Ashitaka and wants to be with him as much as possible. They have time to work things out."[33] For them, at least, their love is redemptive.

Like *Nausicaa, Princess Mononoke* is an antiwar film, yet the depiction of violence in the latter is more nuanced and painful. Nonviolent purity is no longer so simple. Nausicaa stops a war, but Ashitaka cannot. Now violence and its consequences are not so easy to escape. Nausicaa repeatedly confronts attackers without fighting back, but Ashitaka has to fight to stop the fighting. At the beginning of *Nausicaa*, our heroine is able to calm a crazed Ohmu who is attacking Yupa. At the beginning of *Mononoke*, Ashitaka tries to calm a crazed boar-god who is attacking his village, but he is unsuccessful and has to kill it. Ashitaka himself is cursed by this act, and it does not help that his wound was earned in defense of his own people. His maddened victim (poisoned by an iron pellet from Lady Eboshi's gun, we learn later) gives him a wound that will destroy him. In the meantime, however, Ashitaka's curse encourages him to kill more and enables him to kill better—a poignant metaphor for the addictive cycle of reciprocal violence passed down from one victim to another.

All the main characters are scarred by their own violence, but the nastiest person in *Mononoke* turns out to be Jiko, a disarmingly charming itinerant priest and secret agent for the unseen emperor. Jiko is willing to betray Irontown and evidently anyone else to get what he wants, yet he is not evil per se, just selfish and ignorant of the consequences of his actions for others. For him as for them, the ends justify the means. Others kill and deceive to promote their own group interests, while he does it to promote his own interest, so he is not really much different from anyone else.

This complicated and subtle plot begs to be contrasted with the usual sort of animated film—for example, Disney's *The Lion King*, which was shown in Japanese cinemas about the same time. *The Lion King* contrasts the noble ruler of the animals, his loving wife, and their innocent cub Simba—all good, of course—with Simba's evil uncle. The evil uncle hatches a plot to kill the king and eliminate Simba, who escapes but eventually returns to fight the uncle, et cetera. All very predictable, if often beautiful visually.

The basic problem with such plots is that, although they are repetitious to the point of boredom, we nevertheless tend to love them, because this struggle between good (those we identify with) and evil (the others) is so comfortable, so satisfying, so reassuring. The myth of redemptive violence is extraordinarily attractive, often irresistible, because it is a simple way to make sense of our messy world. Think of the plot of every James Bond film, every Star Wars film, every Indiana Jones film, every Terminator film, and now every Harry Potter film. The bad guys are caricatures: ruthless, maniacal, without remorse, they must be stopped by any means necessary. We are meant to feel that it is okay—but let's tell the truth: it is quite pleasurable—to see violence inflicted upon them. Because the villains like to hurt people, it is okay to hurt them in return. Because they like to kill people, it is okay to kill them. After all, they are evil, and evil must be destroyed.

What is this kind of story really teaching us? That if you want to hurt someone, you must demonize them first: that is, fit them into your good-versus-evil script. So even school bullies usually begin by looking for some petty offense (often a perceived insult) that they can use to justify their own violence. Unfortunately, this script remains all too common in modern war and politics too. During the Cold War, capitalist and socialist countries demonized each other; more recently, Islamic fundamentalists demonize the West ("America the Great Satan") and vice-versa. As usual, the first casualty of all such conflicts is truth: states and other groups use the media to "sell" their script to people.

Such scripts presuppose and reinforce the delusion of a self (whether individual ego or collective "wego") whose interests are promoted at the cost of the "not-self," of whatever is outside oneself and therefore can be used as the means to one's own ends. That the underlying problem is with self becomes clear when we ask: who or what does each character in the films identify with? Violence occurs because the benefits for one's own group are pursued at the cost of other groups, but Nausicaa and Ashitaka do not play that game. Because they identify with everyone, including the animals who inhabit the natural world, they refuse to exploit any group for the sake of another. This frees them from the narrow-minded resentment and violent tendencies that the others express. They show us another way.

Fear versus Love

According to Buddhism, the three poisons of greed, ill will, and delusion must be transformed into generosity, loving-kindness, and wisdom, in order to overcome our own and others' suffering. Nausicaa and Ashitaka embody such a transformation, but can we say something more about this alternative? We conclude with a few reflections on the other mode of being they exemplify.

In place of the usual good-versus-evil duality, both films point toward a more insightful distinction between two basic modes of *being in the world,* which are two different ways of responding to the impermanence and insecurity of our life in the world. One mode involves trying to control the world we are in, to make it less threatening and more amenable to our will. The Pejitean ruler Kushana in *Nausicaa* and Lady Eboshi in *Mononoke* are obvious examples, although this mode also applies to many other characters in both films.

The other mode involves a very different strategy: opening ourselves up to the world in a way that does not allow our concern for controlling the world to dominate the way we respond to it.

Both of these ways of living involve a quest for security, but they seek that security in different ways, because they understand the nature and source of security differently. *Security* is from the Latin *se + cura,* literally "without care." To live without care means that our lives are not preoccupied with worrying about our lives. We can try to achieve such a condition by completely controlling our world, as Kushana and Eboshi try to do, yet there are other ways to be "without care," which involve a greater trust or faith in the world itself. The first way is more dualistic: we try to manipulate the world in order to fixate our situation and identity. The second way is more nondual: greater openness to the world is possible because it is perceived as less threatening and more welcoming, so our own boundaries can be more permeable. In both *Nausicaa* and *Mononoke* such openness is encouraged because the natural world is depicted as spiritual. It welcomes and heals those humans who enter it with humility and respect. This is also a way to understand the basic teaching of Buddhism. Insofar as we feel separate from the world, we are deluded and we suffer from the consequences of that delusion. Insofar as we realize our interdependence with the world, and live according to that realization, our lives flow more naturally and we become happier.

Both modes of being involve reinforcing feedback systems that tend to incorporate others. As already noticed in Chapter 2, the more we manipulate the world to get what we want, the more we feel separate and alienated from it. Others feel separate from us when we have manipulated them; mutual distrust encourages both sides to manipulate more. On the other hand, the more we can relax, open up to the world, and trust in it, the more we feel a part of it, and the more others feel inclined to trust and open up to us. These feedback loops are exemplified in both films: there are plenty of examples of exploitation leading to resentment and violence, but the way that Nausicaa and Ashitaka try to mediate conflict gradually wins the confidence of combatants on both sides.

Perhaps the best terms for these two modes of being are *fear* and *love*. If these are indeed the two most basic modes of living in the world, the choice between them, or proportion between them, is the basic challenge that confronts each of us as we mature. This choice is nothing new to psychologists, of course, and a contemporary psychotherapist, Mel Schwartz, expresses it superbly: "Contrary to what we may believe there are only two authentic core emotions; they are love and fear. Other emotions are secondary and are typically masks for fear. Of these, anger is very common. Although we may have come to regard anger as a source emotion, it is really a smoke screen for fear. When we look at our anger, we can always find fear buried beneath it. In our culture we are trained to believe that it's unwise to show fear. We erroneously believe that expressing such vulnerability will permit others to take advantage of us. Yet the fear is there nonetheless."[34]

Understanding anger as a mask for fear helps us to understand both films, for fear—of nature, of other groups—is a constant undercurrent. The protagonists display plenty of greed, ill will, and delusion, but it is not difficult to detect the fear that underlies these mind states. *Nausicaa's* plot is driven by the Tolmekian princess Kushana, whose fear of the poisoned forest motivates her to steal a god-warrior to help her destroy it. In an early scene Nausicaa calms her new pet, the fox squirrel Teto, who is ferociously biting her arm: "Don't be afraid.... You were just scared, weren't you?" Later she says the same to Kushana: "What are you so afraid of? You're just like a little fox squirrel." Fear of the poisoned forest fuels the intergroup greed and resentment that Nausicaa refuses to get caught up in.

In *Princess Mononoke* the major conflict is between two powerful women who want to kill each other, because each fears what the other is trying to do. As always, one's own violence is rationalized as defensive, but the hatred and aggression of each becomes a mirror image of the other. During the climactic battle between them, another samurai warlord also attacks Irontown, encouraged by the emperor, who wants Shishigami's head because it can confer immortality. Although this last motivation is not much developed in the film, it reminds us of our greatest fear, perhaps the one that interferes most with our ability to be open to the world.

How does one break out of a cycle of violent retaliation? It is necessary to find ways to address the fear in the heart of the other, yet first we must address the violence in our own hearts by engaging in "internal disarmament" (as the Dalai Lama calls it), to "resist not evil" in the sense of not requiting violence with violence. This does not mean passivity but the type of selfless courage that is not afraid to risk oneself. Classic examples are Shakyamuni Buddha, Christ on the cross ("Forgive them, for they know not what they do"), and more recently Mahatma Gandhi, all emphasizing the ancient law Buddha spoke of, that hatred is never overcome by hatred. Although the *anime* characters Nausicaa and Ashitaka are not quite in the same league, Miyazaki nevertheless offers them as two other exemplars of selfless action. Because *Nausicaa of the Valley of the Winds* and *Princess Mononoke* so vividly bring to life essential Buddhist teachings about violence and compassion, they enlighten us as they entertain us.

The Dharma of
Death and Life

Philip Pullman's *His Dark Materials* and Ursula K. Le Guin's *Earthsea*

Only in silence the word,
only in dark the light,
only in dying life:
bright the hawk's flight
on the empty sky.

—Ursula K. Le Guin

IS IT A COINCIDENCE that the same subterranean theme haunts all the fantasies discussed in the previous chapters?

J. R. R. Tolkien eventually came to believe that *The Lord of the Rings* "is not really about Power and Dominion: that only sets the wheels going; it is about Death and the desire for deathlessness. Which is hardly more than to say it is a tale written by a man!" (*Letters*, 262).

Yet the priority of this theme is not obvious to most readers.

And in Michael Ende's *Momo*, when Momo meets the mysterious Professor Secundus Minutus Hora, she asks him if he is Death.

> The professor smiled. "If people knew the nature of death," he said after a moment's silence, "they'd cease to be afraid of it. And if they ceased to be afraid of it, no one could rob them of their time any more."
>
> "Why not tell them, then?" Momo suggested.
>
> "I already do," said the professor. "I tell them the meaning of death with every hour I send them, but they refuse to listen. They'd sooner heed those who frighten them."[35]

Yet this poignant exchange is not developed any further in Ende's novel.

In Miyazaki's *Nausicaä of the Valley of the Wind* and *Princess Mononoke*, where the focus is on how to break the cycle of violence, death provides a constant context for the fear and revenge that drive the plots. But the reflex of our awareness of death—desire for immortality—enters in a curious way that leads to the climax of *Princess Mononoke*. While everyone else is distracted by the ferocious battles that are raging, Jiko the monk furtively leads a troupe of warriors to kill and behead Shishigami. Why? In an undeveloped part of the story, the emperor—who otherwise plays no role in the tale—seeks the forest god's head because there is a legend that it grants immortality to whoever possesses it.

This chapter looks at two other fantasy series in which death breaks through the surface and becomes the main focus of the story in a highly original way. The first series is the acclaimed *His Dark Materials* trilogy by the British author Philip Pullman, which includes *The Golden Compass, The Subtle Knife,* and *The Amber Spyglass.* Some critics have praised this series as the most important fantasy series since Tolkien's, a view that we do not quite share, for reasons that will become clear later.

The other series, by Ursula Le Guin, and known for almost twenty years as the *Earthsea* trilogy, originally comprised *The Wizard of Earthsea, The Tombs of Atuan,* and *The Farthest Shore.* Much later, however, she added two other novels: *Tehanu* and then *The Other Wind,* along with *Tales from Earthsea,* a collection of short stories dealing with the same world. That the final novels of Pullman's and Le Guin's fantasy series were published almost simultaneously makes their plot parallels—remarkably similar visits to a Hades-like afterlife—all the more striking. Le Guin is better known for her science fiction, especially *The Left Hand of Darkness* and *The Dispossessed,* but to label her as either a children's author or a science fiction author does not do justice to the body of her work, which in the opinion of such critics as Harold Bloom makes her one of America's most important writers. There is certainly much in her tales for Buddhists to appreciate, as we will see.

That Buddhism also focuses on the same concern—fear of death and craving for immortality—is evident in its foundational myth of how Siddhartha, the future Buddha, left his home. According to the legend, Siddhartha was protected from awareness of *dukkha* by being surrounded with young and healthy people. It was only when he insisted on venturing outside the palace grounds that Siddhartha encountered for the first time an old man, an ill man, and a corpse. Later he met an ascetic renouncer, which inspired him to leave the palace and search for a solution to the *dukkha*, the anguish, that confronts all of us.

It makes no difference that this legend seems to be a late addition to the Buddha's biography. The point is that the Buddhist path originated in the Buddha's quest to solve the problem of human *dukkha*—and our greatest *dukkha*, the one that usually terrifies us the most, is our inevitable end. But how can that *dukkha* ever be resolved? We might be able to reduce our anxiety about it, yet that will not keep us from dying. And who wants to die?

Most Christians believe that Christ's death and resurrection have opened the door to heaven for those who embrace him; we should not fear death, since those who live in the right way will enjoy an eternity with God. Some Christian mystics insist that we too must be crucified and reborn, dying to ourselves so that "Not I, but Christ lives in me," as Paul puts it.

In Buddhism, death traditionally means rebirth into another more-or-less frustrating situation, until we realize nirvana—but what that liberation involves is not very clear. Some Buddhists suspect it means annihilation at death, which is why a more comfortable rebirth is often more attractive; canonical Buddhist teachings, however, do not support such an understanding. For those who follow the path of the Buddha, the solution to the *dukkha* of mortality is an "awakening" (the literal meaning of "Buddha") that involves neither annihilation nor some kind of eternal life after death. What happens to a fully-awakened person after death is one of the "unanswered questions" that the Buddha refused as unedifying, because answering it would not be helpful to the questioner's practice. Both annihilationism and eternalism are based on a misunderstanding of the self: there is no self either to be destroyed or to live on forever. Our sense of self is a mental construction that depends upon various physical and psychological factors, including our habitual intentions and automatized responses to situations. According to traditional Buddhist teachings it is these impermanent factors or "habit-energies" that survive physical death and cause rebirth. Previous chapters have pointed out that rebirth has also been understood more metaphorically, as describing what happens moment by moment, as our motivations change.

Life and death can also be seen as another example of the dualistic thinking that usually bedevils us. We emphasize the distinction between them because we want one rather than the other: we cling to life and try to reject or deny death. As with other antithetical concepts, this does not work because the meaning of each is the negation of the other. To be self-conscious—aware that we are alive—is also to be aware of the inevitability of our death, and not necessarily a long time from now. This prospect haunts us, casting a shadow over everything we do or might want to do. What is the meaning of our lives, what is the point of everything, if we will all be dead in a few score years? As the modern world has lost belief in any afterlife or rebirth to sustain us, the question has become more pressing. For most of us it is too distressing to think about, so we repress it into unconsciousness, where it lurks to poison the wellsprings of our creativity and joy.

To be unable to die, then, is to be unable to live. By denying death we also deny life. Yet does this simple way of understanding the problem—life and death are entwined—also contain the seeds of a solution, if we turn it around? Can we learn how to live by learning how to die?

One way to bring these abstract reflections to life is to consider their implications for how we imagine the afterlife. What might the dead themselves tell us about life and death, if we were able to visit them?

Freeing the Dead from Death

Pullman's trilogy is a synthesis that even includes some Buddhist elements, although much of the tale, as well as its overall title, is taken from Milton's *Paradise Lost*. Book II of that epic poem recounts Satan's visit to:

> The womb of nature and perhaps her grave,
> Of neither sea, nor shore, nor air, nor fire,
> But all these in their pregnant causes mixed
> Confusedly, and which thus must ever fight,
> Unless the almighty maker them ordain
> *His dark materials* to create more worlds,
> Into this wild abyss the wary fiend [Satan]
> Stood on the brink of hell and looked a while,
> Pondering his voyage...   (lines 911-919, italics added)

William Blake noticed that, fiend or not, Satan is the most interesting character in *Paradise Lost*, and he concluded that Milton "was
of the devil's party without knowing it." Pullman, another member
of the devil's party, ordains his own dark materials to create more
worlds, in his case a vast "multiverse" with many parallel worlds
including a heaven almost as unattractive as hell. In so doing he
turns the Biblical story upside down. In place of the fall from grace,
which led to our expulsion from the Garden of Eden, Pullman offers
an updated, more secular version in which humanistic grace tri-
umphs over superstition and ignorance. *His Dark Materials* has
much more to say about religion than any of the other fantasies discussed in this book—and most of it is negative. Many Buddhists,
especially Western converts disillusioned with Christianity, will find
his attack on institutionalized religion incisive, and enjoy his barbs
at those who speak on behalf of "the Authority, God, the Creator,
the Lord, Yahweh, El, Adonai, the King, the Father, the Almighty."[36]
But does Pullman end up throwing the spiritual baby out along with
the dogmatic, authoritarian bath water of organized monotheism?

The plot of each book is much too complex to summarize briefly,
so what follows is no more than a rough outline highlighting the
main line of development while ignoring all the subplots that make
the whole so rich and compelling. The first novel, *The Golden
Compass,* tells the story of Lyra Belacqua, a free-spirited child raised
(more or less unsupervised) by the scholars of Oxford's hallowed
Jordan College, who ends up traveling to the far north on a quest
to save a kidnapped friend. Her parallel world is different from ours
in some curious ways. Everyone is born with a *daemon*, a kind of

spirit-animal that always stays with them because it is part of them,
apparently a representation of their own spirit. Also, although Lyra's
world is technologically modern in many ways, the Protestant
Reformation evidently never occurred, leaving everyone subject to
a monolithic, all-powerful Church that does not hesitate to ferret
out nonconformists and persecute any whiff of heresy.

When Lyra's friend Roger is abducted by the mysterious
"Gobblers," she embarks on a search that involves adventures with
Gyptian boat people, Scandinavian witches, and the exiled king of
the armored bears of the North. In the climax, she encounters her
estranged parents, Lord Asriel and Mrs. Coulter, who are conduct-
ing mystical/scientific investigations into "Dust," a mysterious substance whose importance only gradually becomes clear in the later
books. Lyra discovers that their research involves one of the most horrific experiments conceivable: separating kidnapped children from
their daemons, which kills both child and daemon. At the shocking
conclusion, when her father does this to her childhood friend Roger
and his daemon, we learn that the burst of energy released in this process can be used to create an opening into a parallel world. Her apparently evil father goes through this hole, in order to discover the
secret of Dust. In the last paragraph Lyra tries to follow him.

The Subtle Knife begins in our world with Will Parry, a scared boy
on the run after he accidentally kills a man while protecting his
mother. He flees to Oxford, where he stumbles through a "window" into the streets of Cittàgazze in a parallel universe. There he
meets Lyra, who has also fallen into that world. The city is haunted
by gruesome Specters, invisible spirits who eat the souls of adults

while leaving children alone until they are "ripe." Will discovers that he is destined to be the bearer of the "subtle knife," a dagger that can cut windows between the millions of worlds, and the two use it to travel back and forth from Will's world to Lyra's, as well as to others. They are pursued and find themselves the focus of a momentous struggle between the forces of good and evil. While the charming Mrs. Coulter seems to be deceiving people on both sides, Lord Asriel is forming an army to wage war on heaven. But who is really good, and who is evil?

The Amber Spyglass, the concluding novel, tells of the great war in heaven between "the Authority" and the forces of Lord Asriel, while Lyra and Will seek the land of the dead to comfort the soul of her friend Roger. This is where the story becomes quite intriguing from a Buddhist perspective, and there are even some Buddhist allusions. Lyra and Will visit a Tibetan-type community in the Himalayan mountains, complete with prayer flags, a monastery, and a wise healer named Pagdzin Tulku. They also discover that God is a fraud. A guardian angel named Balthamos, who is in the know, informs them:

> "The Authority, God, the Creator, the Lord, Yahweh, El, Adonai, the King, the Father, the Almighty—these were all the names he gave himself. He was never the creator. He was an angel like ourselves—the first angel, true, the most powerful, but he was formed of Dust as we are, and Dust is only a name for what happens when matter begins to understand itself, and Dust is formed. The first angels condensed out of Dust, and the Authority was the first of all. He told those who came after him that

he had created them, but it was a lie. One of those who came later was wiser than he was, and she found out the truth, so he banished her." (28)

Here Pullman reveals some familiarity with Buddhism, for this is an amusing adaptation of a story given in the Brahmajala Sutra of the Pali Canon, where the Buddha offers what seems to be a humorous parody of Hindu creation myths. When the world contracts, he says, beings are reborn in the Abhassara Brahma world, where they dwell "mind-made, feeding on delight, self-luminous, moving through the air, glorious" for a long time. But eventually one being, having exhausted his life-span or his merits, falls from this Abhassara world and finds himself in an empty Brahma-palace, where he eventually becomes bored, thinking: "Oh, if only some other beings would come here!" And by coincidence, around that same time other Abhassara beings descend in the same way into what is now his Brahma palace, where they become his companions. This leads the first being to think:

"I am Brahma, the Great Brahma, the Conqueror, the Unconquered, the All-Seeing, the All-Powerful, the Lord, the Maker and Creator, Ruler, Appointer and Orderer, Father of All That Have Been and Shall Be. These beings were created by me. How so? Because I first had this thought: 'Oh, if only some other beings would come here!' That was my wish, and then these beings came into this existence!"

But [continues the Buddha] those beings who arose subsequently think: "This, friends, is Brahma, Great Brahma, the Conqueror, the Unconquered, the All-Seeing, the All-Powerful, the Lord, the Maker and Creator, Ruler, Appointer and Orderer, Father of All That Have

Been and Shall Be. How so? We have seen that he was here first, and that we arose after him."

The Buddha goes on to say that beings from that Brahma-palace world might later contract even further and thus descend into our world. Through their powers of concentration they might remember their earlier lives in the Brahma palace and conclude that the same Brahma must have made humans too—but that would just repeat the original mistake.[37]

When we eventually meet "the Almighty" in *The Amber Spyglass,* he turns out to be an old man physically and mentally decrepit, carried around by servants who follow the instructions of Metatron, the powerful regent of heaven with whom Lord Asriel and Mrs. Coulter fight in the climax.

By far the most interesting part of the trilogy, however, is Will and Lyra's visit to the world of the dead. Will wants to meet his dead father again; Lyra hopes to make amends to Roger for the actions of her father, who killed Roger at the conclusion of the first book. By using the subtle knife they eventually find a Hades-like afterworld, where colors leach away as the ghosts of the dead make their way to a lakeside holding area. There Lyra must tearfully separate from her daemon before an aged boatman ferries them to a lifeless, forsaken land on the other side.

Near the wharf Lyra and Will encounter harpies—repulsive birds the size of a vulture, but with a woman's face and breasts—whose shrieking cries frighten them. They flee through a battered wooden door into a vast, misty plain full of adult and child ghosts, standing dully around or lying listlessly on the ground. With no more of their own substance than a fog, the ghosts gather around Lyra and Will, attracted by their life and warmth. "Their voices were no louder than dry leaves falling. And it was only the children who spoke; the adults all seemed sunk in a lethargy so ancient that they might never move or speak again" (266). For the dead nothing ever happens— except torment by the harpies. When they finally find Roger, he tells them the awful truth:

> "This is a terrible place, Lyra, it's hopeless, there's no change when you're dead, and them bird-things…. You know what they do? They wait till you're resting—you can never sleep properly, you just sort of doze—and they come up quiet beside you and they whisper all the bad things you ever did when you was alive, so you can't forget 'em. They know all the worst things about you. They know how to make you feel horrible, just thinking of all the stupid things and bad things you ever did. And all the greedy and unkind thoughts you ever had, they know 'em all, and they shame you up and they make you feel sick with your-self…. But you can't get away from 'em." (275–76)

Later one of the harpies explains how such a hell was created. "Thousands of years ago, when the first ghosts came down here, the Authority gave us the power to see the worst in every one, and we have fed on the worst ever since, till our blood is rank with it and our hearts are sickened" (283). The afterlife is an endless pur-gatory without any possibility of finally expiating for one's sins.

Pullman's afterworld is a powerful metaphor, resonant with im-plications for Buddhism. All the dead end up ruminating forever on all their failures and inadequacies, on their sense of lack. Without the flesh and blood of bodies, however, they lack any opportunity ever to *do* anything about them. As Will says later, "Angels wish they had bodies... angels can't understand why *we* don't enjoy the world more. It would be a sort of ecstasy for them to have our flesh and our senses" (392). This is a repeated theme, especially in the final book. Pullman rejoices in the sensuousness of our bodies, in contrast and in opposition to the Authority's ascetic denial of the senses. And it highlights the ambivalence of the Buddhist tradition, which historically has shared much of the Authority's suspicion of the flesh. Is nirvana the realization of another reality—hence a denial or at least a diminishment of our physicality—or does enlightenment instead awaken us to the true reality of this world, including the true nature of our bodies and their senses?

Buddhist texts can be found to support either understanding. The Buddha taught a Middle Path between asceticism and self-indulgence, a third way which by the religious standards of his time was quite relaxed; by modern standards, however, the discipline of the *sangha* seems quite strict (no sexual contact, no food after noon, no alcohol, no dancing, etc.). Some of the later Mahayana schools of Buddhism, especially the tantric traditions, more clearly affirm our physicality and celebrate the sensuality of an awakened body: the point is not to escape or deny our bodies, but to liberate them from greed, ill will and delusion. How should we understand the difference between these two perspectives?

It helps to remember the cultural context of the Buddha's message, and to emphasize the direction in which he developed the religious tradition into which he had been acculturated. The ascetic practices of his time, which the Buddha himself practiced before the meditations that led to his awakening, involved denial of the senses in an almost mechanical way to accumulate spiritual power, *tapas*. Just as the Buddha revolutionized karma by understanding it in a more ethical fashion that emphasized motivation, so too he revolutionized the religious path by emphasizing the freedom and compassion liberated by spiritual wisdom, instead of the psychic powers that, it was widely believed, could be gained from ascetic denial. For Buddhism, the basic issue is not sin (which is a perversion of the will) but ignorance or delusion (which is a failure in the mind's understanding). The Christian emphasis on will, for example, is often associated with sinful tendencies or weaknesses of the body; the Buddhist emphasis on delusion, in contrast, focuses on psychological hindrances which may or may not affect the body.

The difference is crucial, and toward the end of *The Amber Spyglass* Will and Lyra are initiated into something like the Buddhist perspective: "She [the angel Xaphania] said that all the history of human life has been a struggle between wisdom and stupidity. She and the rebel angels, the followers of wisdom, have always tried to open minds; the Authority and his churches have always tried to keep them closed.... And for most of that time, wisdom has had to work in secret, whispering her words, moving like a spy through the humble places in the world while the courts and palaces are occupied by her enemies" (429). This has certainly been true in Asia, where Buddhist institutions have usually had an uneasy relationship with the state, which tried to appropriate the liberative power of the

Buddhist message to support its own secular power; for example, rulers of Buddhist societies have regularly claimed to be Buddhas or bodhisattvas, while exercising tight control over the *sangha*.

In the midst of a countless host of ghosts, Lyra realizes how she must fulfill the prophecy that she would someday do something great and important in a different world from her own. "What I got to do, Roger, what my destiny is, is I got to help all the ghosts out of the land of the dead forever. Me and Will—we got to rescue you all." She remembers something her father once said: "Death is going to die" (277). Unusually for Pullman, this seems to be a positive allusion to Christianity, specifically the New Testament. In his first letter to the Corinthians, Paul wrote that "The last enemy to be destroyed is death" (1 Cor. 15:26), and *Revelations* declares that in the Last Days "death itself shall die" (Rev. 21:5). But this point has considerable resonance in Buddhism as well: enlightenment is sometimes called "the great death," for the ego-self–that which fears death—must let go and "die," in order for us to be liberated from (the fear of) death.

Will realizes that he can use his knife to cut a window into another world, which everyone can escape through, but the world of the dead is deep underground and every window he tries to make opens onto solid rock. And Will is sick, beginning to weaken. The harpies are starting to close in on them, when the ghost children ask Lyra to tell stories from her life, to help them remember the world they were forgetting.

At the end of her reminiscences, she is startled to realize that the harpies too have silently gathered around her, solemn and spell-bound by her tale. Yet not for long. When they learn of Lyra and

Will's plan to free the dead, the harpies decide to become even more vicious, hurling abuse at every ghost, to make them even more crazy with remorse and self-hatred—but then another possibility arises. Earlier the harpies had become angry and attacked Lyra when she tried to tell them a tall tale, yet they find true stories nourishing because even harpies "desire news of the world and the sun and the wind and the rain." This allows for a new bargain to replace their old contract with the Authority: "Instead of seeing only the wickedness and cruelty and greed of the ghosts that come down here, from now on you will have the right to ask every ghost to tell you the story of their lives, and they will have to tell the truth about what they've seen and touched and heard and loved and known in the world" (317). In return, the harpies agree to guide arriving ghosts to a new window that Will can cut, in a special place they will show him. But those who lie, or hold anything back, or have nothing to tell, *because they have never lived*, will be refused and unable to escape. The psychological implication is astute: those who have never enjoyed their lives are usually the most afraid of death.

The harpies offer to take the travelers to a place where the upper world is close—but then a thin ghost with an angry face asks the obvious question: What will happen when we leave the world of the dead? Will we live again, or evaporate into the air? Lyra consults her alethiometer "truth machine" and reports what it tells her:

"When you go out of here, all the particles that make you up will loosen and float apart, just like your daemons did. If you've seen people dying, you know what that looks like. But your daemons en't just nothing now; they're part of everything. All the atoms that were them, they've gone into the air and the wind and the trees and the earth and all the living things. They'll never vanish. They're just part of everything.... You'll drift apart, it's true, but you'll be out in the open, part of everything alive again." (286)

A few balk at this, but the rest agree with a young woman who had died as a religious martyr, only to discover that the land of the dead is not a place of punishment nor a place of reward, just a place of nothing. "But now this child has come offering us a way out and I'm going to follow her. Even if it means oblivion, friends, I'll welcome it, because it won't be nothing. We'll be alive again in a thousand blades of grass, and a million leaves; we'll be falling in the raindrops and blowing in the fresh breeze; we'll be glittering in the dew under the stars and the moon out there in the physical world, which is our true home and always was" (286–87).

The wish to be part of everything—alive in the grass and glittering in the dew—has no role in traditional Christian conceptions of salvation, yet it is consistent with Buddhist emphasis on interdependence or "interpermeation." To have no self is already to be a part of everything: such nonduality is not a condition to be attained, but an insight to be realized. The Vietnamese Zen teacher and poet Thich Nhat Hanh has expressed this beautifully:

If you are a poet, you will see clearly that there is a cloud floating in this sheet of paper. Without a cloud, there will be no rain; without rain, the trees cannot grow, and without trees we cannot make paper. The cloud is essential for the paper to exist. If the cloud is not here, the sheet of paper cannot be here either....

If we look into this sheet of paper even more deeply, we can see the sunshine in it. If the sunshine is not there, the tree cannot grow. In fact, nothing can grow. Even we cannot grow without sunshine. And so, we know that the sunshine is also in this sheet of paper. The paper and the sunshine inter-are. And if we continue to look, we can see the logger who cut the tree and brought it to the mill to be transformed into paper. And we see the wheat. We know that the logger cannot exist without his daily bread, and therefore the wheat that became his bread is also in this sheet of paper. And the logger's father and mother are in it too....

You cannot point out one thing that is not here—time, space, the earth, the rain, the minerals in the soil, the sunshine, the cloud, the river, the heat. Everything co-exists with this sheet of paper.... As thin as this sheet of paper is, it contains everything in the universe in it.[38]

In a similar fashion, each of us too co-exists with everything in the universe. We do not need to die to become a part of everything, because we already are. This is not the unity of a bowl of oatmeal porridge, in which every spoonful is the same as all the other spoonfuls, but the nonduality of a multifarious world in which each thing is so dependent on everything else that it both contains and is contained by everything else. We are not selves looking out at a world outside us; rather, each of us is what the whole world is doing right here and now. This is not incompatible with the well-known Buddhist claim that all things, including us, are "empty" (Sanskrit, *shunya*).

On the contrary, it is because everything is empty of self-existence that each thing is part of every other thing.

Will and Lyra set off to find a better place to cut a window, led by harpies and followed by an uncountable number of ghosts. After traversing a series of caves and tunnels, with various adventures along the way, Will is able to cut a window that opens onto the sweetest thing any of them had ever seen: a night air fresh and clean, with a canopy of stars overhead and the reflection of water somewhere below. The exodus of the dead begins: "They took a few steps in the world of grass and air and silver light, and looked around, their faces transformed with joy…and held out their arms as if they were embracing the whole universe; and then, as if they were made of mist and smoke, they simply drifted away, becoming part of the earth and the dew and the night breeze" (385–86).

The insubstantial ghosts of the dead are freed, because they are finally able to die and return to the elements (the Dust) of which they are composed. But perhaps such ghosts are not to be found only in the afterlife? Pullman's dead have no sensuous bodies with which to enjoy the world, yet even those with substance often do not know how to appreciate their substance, because of fear. The joy of our bodies is also the problem with our bodies: they are part of the natural world, subject to natural processes, which means they are born and die. That is why those who cannot accept their death have such a hard time accepting their physicality too.

Modern philosophy began with Rene Descartes's mind-body dualism, which can be understood as, among other things, a clever intellectual attempt to evade death. The body cannot really die, he said, because it is only a complicated machine, as mechanical as the rest of the natural world. And our minds, being immaterial, are not susceptible to physical death either. This solution is no longer persuasive to many philosophers, but his formulation expresses our modern sense of alienation from our bodies, an alienation that became more extreme as the world has become more secular, and the secular destiny of our natural bodies more terrifying. This alienation is one way to express our *dukkha* regarding death: the mind looks down at the body, realizes what embodiment means, and panics. For Buddhism, however, the solution is not to try to liberate the mind from the body but to realize their nonduality. The goal is not escaping our embodiment but becoming one with it, without the shadow cast by conceptualizing about life-and-death, in which case we realize that our bodies are quite different from the animated machines we thought they were.

Pullman's particular target is churches that repress our embodiment by labeling it evil. Nevertheless, good stories, as we have noticed, have a way of outgrowing their authors' intentions. Many religious doctrines try to deny our mortality by denying our physicality—"We are souls, not bodies," they insist—yet celebrating our fleshiness, as Pullman does, is not enough unless we are also provided with a solution to the terror that haunts our all-too-mortal flesh. The harpies' demand for true stories means that those who have never lived will be unable to die. But do those who have never lived have the courage to die?

Pullman focuses on our sense of sin. Let go of that conditioning, he says, and enjoy your sensuous embodiment while you can. Don't sacrifice it for some promised pie in the sky after you die. A good point, yet Pullman does not seem to notice that he is fighting a battle that has long since been won, at least for most people. Unfortunately, winning that battle has turned out to be something of a pyrrhic victory. Most people nowadays are obsessed, not with sin and guilt, but with their maxed-out credit cards and their inability to achieve the elusive happiness that the new religion of consumption is supposed to provide. The problem with Pullman's solution to the problem of life—"let's get rid of our sense of sin!"—is that a sense of sin does not by itself explain why we are unable to enjoy our brief time on this earth. The religious game of sin followed by repentance was so compelling because it offered us a solution to death: an eternity with God—at least for those who died without a mortal sin blotting their souls, according to medieval Christian doctrine.

If we are to move beyond the sin-and-repentance story, we need a narrative that does a better job of addressing our terror of death. Buddhism does so obliquely, by translating that game into a different vocabulary. As already discussed in Chapter 3, the Buddhist teaching of *anatta*, or "nonself," implies that the primary issue is not my death sometime in the future but my sense of self right now. The basic problem is that this delusive sense of self feels unreal and ungrounded. Buddhism offers us no way to evade physical death—rebirth just multiplies the problem—yet it does have a solution to our sense of lack: letting go of oneself by "forgetting" oneself. As the Japanese Zen master Dogen put it: "To study the Buddha way is to study the self. To study the self is to forget the self. To forget the self is to be actualized by myriad beings. When actualized by myriad things, your body and mind as well as the body and mind of others drop away. No trace of realizations remains, and this no-trace continues endlessly."[39]

"Forgetting" ourselves is how we lose our sense of separation and realize that we are not other than the world. In Zen meditation, for example, we learn how to forget ourselves, which happens when we become absorbed into our practice. If the self-consciousness of ego is a result of self-reflection—consciousness trying to grasp itself, as it were—meditation is an exercise in which our consciousness *un*-learns trying to grasp itself. Enlightenment occurs when consciousness stops trying to catch its own tail and we let go of ourselves.

In other words, from a Buddhist perspective our problem is not so much death as the ego's inability to let go—not only at the end of our lives, but right here and now—which is also our inability to live. This issue Pullman does not address.

Perhaps inevitably, the rest of the novel is somewhat anticlimactic. There is a ferocious battle between Asriel's forces and those of heaven, led by the regent Metatron, who perishes when he falls into the Abyss clutching Asriel and Mrs. Coulter. It is a convenient plot solution for Lyra's parents, who by the end of the tale are clearly on the side of the good but have done too many evil things along the way to survive and thrive. The great war itself, long anticipated and prepared for, is not much developed and unconvincing when it finally occurs. The plot takes an unexpected and moving twist when Lyra and Will, who have matured into adolescence and fallen in love, discover that they cannot live together. The windows that the subtle knife opens between the worlds turn out to be dangerous because they let precious Dust dissipate, and their own bodies cannot survive for long in each other's world.

By the end, the antireligious enjoy-your-physicality theme has become a bit preachy and less mythically effective. Xaphania uses her revelations about Dust as the occasion to give Lyra and Will a lecture:

> "Dust is not a constant. There's not a fixed quantity that has always been the same. Conscious beings make Dust—they renew it all the time, by thinking and feeling and reflecting, by gaining wisdom and passing it on. And if you help everyone else in your worlds to do that, by helping them to learn and understand about themselves and each other and the way everything else works, and by showing them how to be kind instead of cruel, and patient instead of hasty, and cheerful instead of surly, and above all how to keep their minds open and free and curious..." (440–41)

And so forth. Xaphania's values are admirable, to be sure, and more than compatible with Buddhist precepts for ethical conduct, but the task of fiction is to bring those virtues to life by depicting them in a way that speaks to our own lives, rather than by lecturing about them.

Pullman's tendentiousness seems to be a consequence of making religion the focus of the story rather than fully integrating a spiritual perspective into the tale. Pullman is so focused on criticizing the theistic sin-and-guilt story that his own alternative myth about how to live never quite comes to life, except as a reaction to the one he rejects. The negativity of his critique tends to overshadow his more provocative insight into the relationship between our life and our death.

For a more satisfying exploration of the same theme, including some remarkably similar visits to the world of the dead, we turn to Ursula Le Guin's *Earthsea* novels. From our Buddhist perspective, these novels provide perhaps the most profound and moving fantasy series of our time.

Breaking the Wall Between Life and Death

Earthsea is a water world, a collection of islands with different societies and languages. Le Guin is a master at weaving such intercultural narratives: her parents were the anthropologist A. L. Kroeber and the writer Theodora Kroeber, well known for (among other things) their study of Ishi, the last surviving Yahi Indian whom they befriended and protected. Le Guin's own anthropological sensibility enables her to explore the different perspectives that arise when worlds intersect. Investigation of another culture reveals much about one's own, and many of her stories skillfully employ this device to defamiliarize our world and reflect upon it.

The people of Earthsea live in premodern, mostly agricultural societies, with hereditary rulers and seafaring merchants in the coastal towns. Magic performs the role of our technology; wizardry is a respected and needed skill, although not all mages are equally skillful or trustworthy. In *The Wizard of Earthsea*, the first novel, we meet the young goatherd Sparrowhawk, later known as Ged, whose aptitude for magic is revealed when he defends his village against an enemy attack. After his aunt, a witch, teaches him all her charms and spells, he goes to the famous School for Wizards on Roke Island. There his skill rapidly develops, along with his pride, which tempts him to challenge certain dangerous powers before he is fully equipped to deal with them. The consequence is that Ged lets loose an evil shadow-beast into the world, one that he alone can subdue. The rest of the novel is his quest to do so.

He first encounters the shadow-beast when he uses his magic too arrogantly in trying to save a dying child. Attempting to bring the child back to the realm of life, he follows it too far into the realm of death and finds himself alone on a dark hillside. "The stars did not move. No wind blew over the dry steep ground. In all the vast kingdom of the darkness only he moved, slowly, climbing. He came to the top of the hill, and saw the low wall of stones there. But across the wall, facing him, there was a shadow" (95). The shapeless shadow whispers at him and reaches toward him, but as he tries to attack it with his spirit-staff a blinding light knocks him unconscious. When the scarred Ged recovers he discovers that the shadow has escaped from the land of death into Earthsea. It awaits the opportunity to attack him again and eat him from inside.

Terrified, Ged flees from one island to another, until he realizes that he must confront the shadow-beast. But when he tries to approach it, the shadow wavers, then turns and flees, unable to draw on Ged's own power, now that Ged no longer runs away from it. The chase extends to the far corners of Earthsea, where they have their inevitable confrontation: "At first it was shapeless, but as it drew nearer it took on the look of a man. An old man it seemed, grey and grim, coming towards Ged; but even as Ged saw his father the smith in that figure, he saw that it was not an old man but a young one." It turns into Jasper, his enemy at the School of Wizardry. It becomes in turn the different people he has feared, before sloughing off all human form as it continued to approach. Crawling on four short taloned legs upon the sand, it heaved itself upright before Ged:

> In silence, man and shadow met face to face, and stopped.
>
> Aloud and clearly, breaking that old silence, Ged spoke the shadow's name, and in the same moment the shadow spoke without lips or tongue, saying the same word: "Ged." And the two voices were one voice.
>
> Ged reached out his hands, dropping his staff, and took hold of his shadow, of the black self that reached out to him. Light and darkness met, and joined, and were one.

At first his companion, Vetch, is terrified that Ged has been overcome, but then "he began to see the truth, that Ged had neither lost nor won but, naming the shadow of his death with his own name, had made himself whole: a man: who, knowing his whole true self, cannot be used or possessed by any power other than himself, and whose life is therefore lived for life's sake and never in the service of ruin, or pain, or hatred, or the dark."[40]

Ged's magic had been useless against the shadow because he had not known its true name, which at the end is revealed to be none other than his own. The shadow is not only his death but his fear of death, which is why it attacked and chased him. Our (fear of) death pursues us until we turn to face it and realize that it is nondual with our life. That realization is rarely an easy one, which is why it involves a spiritual quest. Terror of death also lies at the root of our capacity for evil, the latter summoned by Ged's misuse of his magical powers. If we understand that our death is not opposed to our life, and therefore not to be feared and rejected, we become whole, integrating those anti-death (and therefore anti-life) tendencies within us that sometimes motivate us to scapegoat others. We thereby free ourselves from subordination to other powers that would use us to deny life, as well as from our own inclinations to hurt or take advantage of others.

In *The Tombs of Atuan*, the second novel, Ged has become famous as the Archemage of all the islands, but the story focuses on Arha, a young girl who, because she was born on the same day that the previous Great Princess died, is destined to become the new Priestess Tenar of the Tombs of Atuan. As this suggests, there are some similarities with Tibetan Buddhism, whose most important teachers are also believed to be reborn, the most well-known being the Dalai Lama and the Panchen Lama. In this novel, however, Le Guin presents us with the cruel, negative image of a religion based on reincarnation, in which the emphasis is on exercising power rather than expressing compassion. Tenar learns the elaborate rituals of the Nameless Ones and the secrets of the Great Labyrinth hidden under the tombs, where no man can enter. Yet Ged does enter, seeking the lost half of the Ring of Erreth-Akbe, which must be restored to crown a king who can bring peace to the feuding islands. He is trapped in the labyrinth, but gradually he wins the trust of the young princess by revealing different values from the ones she has been taught. Together they escape just before the tombs crumble into the desert sands.

The Farthest Shore crowns Le Guin's original trilogy, with a longer visit to the land of the dead and a deeper meditation on the meaning of death for life. Young Arren, Prince of Enlad, has come to Roke where the master wizards live, with disquieting news from the western islands. The Equilibrium seems to be failing, for some unknown evil power is sapping the roots of life and threatening the harmony of the world. He and the Archemage, Ged, set off to track down this evil, visiting remote islands where the inhabitants have become confused and spells no longer work. Ged realizes what threatens them:

> "Nature is not unnatural. This is not a righting of the balance, but an upsetting of it. There is only one creature who can do that."
>
> "A man?" Arren said, tentative.
>
> "We men."
>
> "How?"
>
> "By an unmeasured desire for life."
>
> "For life? But it isn't wrong to want to live?"
>
> "No. But when we crave power over life—endless wealth, unassailable safety, immortality—then desire becomes greed. And if knowledge allies itself to that greed, then comes evil. Then the balance of the world is swayed, and ruin weighs heavily in the scale." (128)

Their adventures include many encounters with people who are dying or mad, including Arren himself who becomes deluded for a while. They nearly perish when their boat runs out of fresh water, but are rescued by the Children of the Open Sea, raft-dwelling folk who never walk on land. Arren begins to learn about death and, from death, about life.

"I was a child when I began this voyage. I did not believe in death. I have learned something, not much maybe but something. I have learned to believe in death. But I have not learned to rejoice over it, to welcome my death, or yours. If I love life shall I not hate the end of it?"...

"Life without end," the mage said. "Life without death. Immortality. Every soul desires it, and its health is the strength of its desire.... And then—this. This blight upon the lands.... No births; no new lives. No children. Only what is mortal bears life, Arren. Only in death is there rebirth. The Balance is not a stillness. It is a movement—an eternal becoming." (150–51)

Eventually they learn that the cause of the cosmic disturbance is Cob, a necromancer highly skilled at summoning the dead yet also terrified of his own death. They sail through the Western Run to the shores of Selidor, where they wander into the hills looking for him. After a long aimless day, dread and weariness make Arren burst out: "This land is as dead as the land of death itself."

"Do not say that," the mage said sharply. He strode on a while and then went on, in a changed voice, "Look at this land; look about you. This is your kingdom, the kingdom of life. This is your immortality. Look at the hills, the mortal hills. They do not endure forever. The hills with the living grass on them, and the streams of water running.... In all the world, in all the worlds, in all the immensity of time, there is no other like each of those streams, rising cold out of the earth where no eye sees it, running through the sunlight and the darkness to the sea. Deep are the springs of being, deeper than life, than death." (181)

Then Arren sees the world through his companion's eyes, perceiving "the living splendour that was revealed about them in the silent, desolate land, as if by a power of enchantment surpassing any other, in every blade of the wind-bowed grass, every shadow, every stone. So when one stands in a cherished place for the last time before a voyage without return, he sees it all whole, and real, and dear, as he has never seen it before and never will see it again" (182).

They begin to encounter ghosts of the dead, summoned back to this world by Cob, "all with sad, staring faces. They seemed to speak, but Arren could not hear their words, only a kind of whispering blown away by the west wind" (182). They descend into the land of the dead, where no wind ever blows and unwinking stars never move, stepping over the wall of stones and walking down a hillside into one of its cities. All whom they saw stood still, or moved about aimlessly, their faces showing neither anger nor hope. "Instead of fear, then, great pity rose up in Arren, and if fear underlay it, it was not for himself, but for us all. For he saw the mother and child who had died together; but the child did not run, nor did it cry, and the mother did not hold it, nor even look at it. And those who had died for love passed each other in the streets" (189–90).

We are reminded of Pullman's ghosts, sunk in an ancient lethargy, with no more substance than a fog and voices no louder than dry leaves falling. Ged and Arren continue through the city and into a rocky valley, where they finally encounter Cob, who boasts to them that he now has no fear. "What should a dead man fear?" he asks, but his laugh rings false.

> "I do not know what a dead man should fear," Ged answered, "Surely not death? Yet it seems you fear it. For you have found a way to escape from it."
>
> "I have. I live: my body lives…. I who alone among all the mages found the Way of Immortality, which no other ever found!"
>
> "Maybe we did not seek it," said Ged.
>
> "You sought it. All of you. You sought it and could not find it, and so made wise words about acceptance and balance and the equilibrium of life and death. But they were words—lies to cover your failure—to cover your fear of death! What man would not live forever, if he could? And I can. I am immortal. I did what you could not do…. I made a spell— the greatest spell that has ever been made. The greatest and the last!"
>
> "In working that spell, you died."
>
> "Yes! I died. I had the courage to die, to find what you cowards could never find—the way back from death. I opened the door that had been shut since the beginning of time. And now I come freely to this place, and freely return to the world of the living. Alone of all men in all time I am the Lord of the Two Lands. And the door I opened is open not only here, but in the minds of the living, in the depths and unknown places of their being, where we are all one in the darkness." (184–86)

Cob's spell has disturbed the Equilibrium, the harmony of
Earthsea, by rupturing the barrier between the world of the living
and the world of the dead. Patiently Ged probes and questions Cob's
ability to summon up the shadows of the dead, even that of Lord
Erreth-Akbe, the greatest hero of Earthsea's past. He explains to
Cob that his solution to death is a failure.

"Did you not understand that he [Erreth-Akbe], even he, is but a
shadow and a name? His death did not diminish life. Nor did it diminish him. He is there—*there*, not here! Here is nothing, dust and shadows. There, he is the earth and sunlight, the leaves of trees, the eagle's
flight. He is alive. And all who ever died, live; they are reborn, and have
no end, nor will there ever be an end. All, save you. For you would not
have death. You lost death, you lost life, in order to save yourself. Yourself!
Your immortal self! What is it? Who are you?"

"I am myself. My body will not decay and die—"

"A living body suffers pain, Cob; a living body grows old; it dies.
Death is the price we pay for our life, and for all life.... You sold the
green earth and the sun and stars to save yourself. But you have no self.
All that which you sold, that is yourself. You have given everything for
nothing. And so now you seek to draw the world to you, all that light and
life you lost, to fill up your nothingness. But it cannot be filled. Not all
the songs of earth, not all the stars of heaven, could fill your emptiness."
(197–98)

"Cob" is an old word for spider, and Cob is finally caught in the
web that he himself has spun. Although fear and hatred keep him

from cooperating, he cannot deny the truth of Ged's words. Despairing, he flees, but they follow him to the door between the worlds, which his spell had opened but he cannot shut. It is a gaping black hole beneath a tumbling cliff. Ged uses all his skill and strength to close it, and with the greatest difficulty he is just able to manage it. Thus they succeed in restoring the world's Equilibrium, although at a terrible price: Ged has exhausted all his magical powers, which are lost forever.

Cob's body is never found, but what about all those other ghosts still languishing in the cities of the dead? What Authority created their endless purgatory? And how might they be liberated from it? *The Farthest Shore* does not address these questions, which must wait until the final Earthsea book.

Seventeen years later Le Guin published another Earthsea novel, *Tehanu*, with a very different mood. The central character is the former High Priestess Tenar, rescued from the Tombs of Atuan, later married to a farmer, and now widowed. The times are bad again. Evil is growing and perversions of magic are becoming more common. Ged appears only late in the story, transported back to Gont on the back of a dragon, but ill and embarrassed by his loss of magic powers. A more important figure is Therru, an abused little girl hideously disfigured by a fire, whom Tenar rescues and protects from her persecutors. Gradually Tenar draws her out and together they struggle to make sense of the world that is changing around them. At the climax Ged and Tenar, now a couple, are captured by an evil mage called Erisen, who humiliates them and is about to kill them when Therru unexpectedly summons a dragon. The dragon saves them and acknowledges the mysterious child as a shape-shifted dragon whose true name is Tehanu.

The plot is slow and almost irrelevant, the climax forced and awkward. A minor key of almost melancholic contemplation pervades the story, in a spare, precise prose that evokes as much as it describes. Some read it as a feminist novel because of its strong female characters, but this is the Earthsea book favored least by many readers, including us.

In contrast, *The Other Wind,* published eleven years after *Tehanu,* provides a fitting conclusion to the whole saga—we feel confident in saying "a conclusion" because it is hard to imagine what could follow this tour de force. Ged, still without any magic powers, again plays a marginal role, while the focus returns to the land of the dead, and to the forlorn shadows stranded there. To supplement the reflections on life and death, another theme is developed. We have learned that to live we must be able to die; now we learn that in order to die we must be able to love.

Ged's little homestead on Gont is visited by Alder, a young sorcerer skilled at the minor spells of mending. He comes to ask Ged's help, for he is haunted by dreams that will not let him rest. His beloved wife Lily, who died in childbirth along with their baby, has been appearing in his dreams. In them, she stands on the slope of a hill beyond a low stone wall, where unblinking stars never move and the wind never blows—an obvious reference to the land of the dead that Ged and Arren visited in the third novel. Lily reaches out over the wall to Alder saying, "Set me free!" This dream recurs whenever Alder sleeps, but now it is not just his wife but a crowd of the dead who every night call out to him, "Set us free!" Alder knows that Ged has visited the land of the dead, and hopes that he may know what to do. Ged, however, has no power to help and sends him to join Tenar and Tehanu. They are on the island of Havnor with King Lebannen, who was formerly Ged's apprentice Arren.

Lebannen welcomes Arren and understands his problem, for similar nightmares are beginning to infect the dreams of many people. But there are other difficulties as well, especially the dangerous matter of dragons who have begun to stray from their traditional territory in the far west, harrying people and burning buildings.

In response to an appeal from Tehanu, a dragon appears and shape-shifts into a young woman named Irian, who explains what the problem is. Some of the young dragons are upset that humans long ago stole half their realm and made "walls of spells" to keep them out of it. Until now the older dragons have been able to control the younger ones. "But not for long. And they fear nothing in the world, except your wizardries of death." Lebannen is puzzled, for by reputation dragons fear nothing at all. Irian answers bluntly: "We fear your spells of immortality.... You have unmade the balance of the world. Can you restore it?"[41]

Since Cob and his necromancy are long gone, no one understands what she is talking about. Tehanu, however, suggests that they all need to go to the Immanent Grove on Roke, the center of things and the most sacred place in the islands. "For it may be that the balance of power within the Archipelago, as well as the Equilibrium of the whole, is in question." And so they sail together to the Isle of the

Wizards, where they meet with the greatest mages of Earthsea for the unexpected denouement.

On board ship, Alder complains to his friend, the wizard Seppel: "Death breaks the bond of soul with body, and the body dies. It goes back to the earth. But the spirit must go to that dark place, and wear a semblance of the body, and endure there—for how long? Forever? In the dust and dark where, without light, or love, or cheer at all? I cannot bear to think of Lily in that place. Why must she be there? Why can she not be—" his voice stumbled, "be free?"

"Because the wind does not blow there," Seppel said. "It was stopped from blowing, by the art of man" (188–89).

Alder does not yet understand but soon he will. Everyone has anxious dreams the night before they arrive; the disturbance is getting worse. Once they are gathered within the Immanent Grove, the Summoner acknowledges that a serious problem has arisen with the boundaries between life and death. Yet he doubts that dragons from the west can be trusted to help solve it, nor eastern peoples "who foreswore their immortal souls when they forgot the Language of the Making," the language of sorcery that uses the original names of things. Tenar, who is from one of the eastern islands, bristles at this: "You are not immortal.... *We* are! We die to rejoin the undying world. It was you who foreswore immortality" (222–23). Peoples of the East are suspicious of wizardry because they believe that immortality is gained only by returning to the earth, to be born again as different beings in different form.

Irian again speaks for the dragons: "Men fear death as dragons do not. Men want to own life, possess it, as if it were a jewel in a box.

Those ancient mages craved everlasting life. They learned to use true names to keep men from dying. But those who cannot die can never be reborn" (225–26). The rest of the novel reverberates with the shockwaves of this revelation, which challenges the original foundations of Earthsea wizardry.

It is curious that our primary metaphor for mortality (nature, whose creatures die) is also our primary metaphor for immortality (the natural world of continuous rebirth). Leaves shrivel and drop in autumn, yet branches bud again in spring. Our problem is not that there is no rebirth, for the cycle of birth and death never ceases, but that we ourselves—our selves—are not reborn. For Buddhists who understand and accept that they have never had a self, that should not be a problem. Is this a better way to understand Buddhist rebirth today? Insofar as we have never had or been a self that could die, death is the condition for our own as well as the world's renewal. In dying we give all our unfulfilled possibilities back to the earth, for the earth to live them out in another way. Is it only by dying, then, that we achieve immortality? Such a metaphorical interpretation of rebirth does not necessarily imply a rejection of more literal understandings, yet it does not require us to make a leap of faith into a belief that many find implausible today.

Long ago, we finally learn, humans and dragons had been of the same kind, speaking one language, but they sought different things and so agreed to part. Men went east, dragons west. In exchange for forgoing wizardry and forgetting the language of sorcery, humans received skill of hand and all that hands can make, while the dragons abandoned such things in favor of the fire of sunlight and the freedom to ride the wind. Then humans broke the covenant. One of the Roke wizards explains how the ancient Rune Makers had become jealous of the dragons' realm,

> "That they could fly.... outside of time, it may be.... And envying that freedom, they followed the dragons' way into the west beyond the west. There they claimed part of that realm as their own. A timeless realm, where the self might be forever. But not in the body, as the dragons were. Only in spirit could men be there.... So they made a wall which no living being could cross, neither man nor dragon.... And their arts of naming laid a great net of spells upon all the western lands, so that when the people of the islands die, they would come to the west beyond the west and live there in the spirit forever.
>
> "But as the wall was built and the spell laid, the wind ceased to blow, within the wall. The sea withdrew. The springs ceased to run. The mountains of sunrise became the mountains of the night. Those that died came to a dark land, a dry land." (227–28)

Afraid to die, men had used wizardry to create a timeless realm, but a timeless realm is a dead realm. It turned out that such immortality is a poor imitation of the true eternity enjoyed by dragons, who are free forever because they live in the now.

Not everyone sees the point. According to the Summoner, Cob's spells must still be the cause of the disturbance. "And so the souls of the dead come reaching now across the wall, yearning back to life."

In response, Alder stands up to speak the truth that they are now able to recognize: "It is not life they yearn for. It is death. To be one with the earth again. To rejoin it."

He asks Tehanu to go down into the dark with him and help tear down the stone wall that confines the ghosts of the dead. Later Lebannen, Irian, and the wizards join them. Although he has lost his mending powers, Alder is recognized as their leader because of his great love. In fact, following his heart makes him a greater healer than ever. Together they are able to push the stones aside, and hear a vast, soft cry from the host of shadows on the other side, who crowd toward them.

> Most came forward afoot. They were not pressing, not crying out now, but walking with unhurried certainty toward the fallen places in the wall: great multitudes of men and women, who as they came to the broken wall did not hesitate but stepped across it and were gone: a wisp of dust, a breath that shone an instant in the ever-brightening light.
>
> Alder watched them.... At last he saw her among them. He tossed the stone aside then and stepped forward. "Lily," he said. She saw him and smiled and held out her hand to him. He took her hand and they crossed together into the sunlight. (239)

And disappeared into it. The scarred Tehanu is transformed into a magnificent dragon blazing fire, and flies away, while Tenar sings: "O my joy, be free...." The Equilibrium is restored. Tenar returns to Ged on Roke, where they tend their garden and goats.

The Other Wind is so moving and mythic because Earthsea is not much different from our world. Earthsea's wizardry is similar to our modern technology. Both are used to control and deny death, and both are motivated by an inability to embrace the type of immortality available to us. Like Ged, who goes too far trying to save a dying child, our sophisticated medical technologies attempt to preserve life by any means necessary. For Earthsea's wizards as for us, death is failure. Yet neither sorcery nor technology works as intended; both backfire, creating unexpected problems. "The goal of wizardry was to triumph over time and live forever.... But we built it wrong" (232). The badly damaged biosphere reminds us that we have wrought no better.

Who are our shades of the dead that cry out "Set us free!" from the other side of the wall? Our culture too is haunted by ghosts: those who are unable to live, either because they are paralyzed by their dread of death or because they compulsively chase after symbolic tokens of immortality such as money, fame, and power. We too are sleeping less well recently, for our dreams have assumed a cumulative life of their own and now return as our nightmares—not all of which happen while we sleep.

At the beginning of the story, we think that the low stone wall is a barrier between life on this side and death on the other. But the dead are not really dead, for the wall was erected to deny death by preserving a timeless, immortal realm for them. At the end, we realize that life and death are both on this side of the wall, while on the other side the ghosts of the dead are trapped in a limbo where nothing ever happens. As Will and Lyra also discover, the dead cry out to die, for their death promises a return to the nondual realm of life-and-death. "What was built is broken. What was broken is made whole" (240). Building the wall broke the natural unity of life and death. Breaking down the wall restores it.

Buddhism also denies that wall, and the Middle Path gives us another way to break it down. For Dogen, the clarification of "birth and death" is the most important issue of all—*birth* and death, not life and death, reminding us that birth, not life, is the opposite of death. In the "Shinjin-gakudo" (Body-and-Mind Study of the Way) section of his *Shobogenzo,* however, he denies that they are really opposites: "Not abandoning birth, you see death. Not abandoning death, you see birth. Birth does not hinder death. Death does not hinder birth.... Death is not the opposite of birth; birth is not the opposite of death."[42]

We should not try to hold on to one while pushing the other away. To affirm one is to affirm both. In the "Shoji" (Birth and Death) section Dogen emphasizes that we should not look for a liberation that involves transcending birth and death:

> If you search for a Buddha outside birth and death, it will be like... trying to see the Big Dipper while you are facing south; you will cause yourself to remain all the more in birth and death and lose the way of emancipation.
>
> Just understand that birth-and-death is itself nirvana. There is nothing such as birth and death to be avoided; there is nothing such as nirvana to be sought. Only when you realize this are you free from birth and death.[43]

Enlightenment is not about realizing some other realm or dimension apart from birth and death, but about awakening to their true nature. Liberation is to be found in, or rather *as,* birth and death.

Finally, and most enigmatically, the *Shoji* section goes on to say that because birth does not *become* death, birth is experienced as no-birth, and death as no-death:

> It is a mistake to suppose that birth turns into death. Birth is a phase that is an entire period of itself, with its own past and future. For this reason, in buddha-dharma birth is understood as no-birth. Death is a phase that is an entire period of itself, with its own past and future. For this reason, death is understood as no-death.
>
> In birth there is nothing but birth and in death there is nothing but death. Accordingly, when birth comes, face and actualize birth, and when death comes, face and actualize death. Do not avoid them or desire them.[44]

To understand this, we must again remember *anatta,* the Buddhist claim that there is no self and never was. There is only a delusive *sense of self* that clings to life because it is terrified of death, but that can awaken to its true nature by letting go of itself. What does this imply about birth and death? If there is no real self that is born, then there is only the act of birth. Yet our usual understanding of birth assumes that something is born; if nothing—no *thing*—is born then the term loses its usual meaning. If there is only the act of birth, then there is really no birth—just the act, the process of birthing, each moment, each breath, each push, each pain whole and complete in itself, lacking nothing and gaining nothing. Then birth is no-birth.

Exactly the same is true for death. If there is no self that dies, then there is only the process of dying, with nothing to hold on to and nothing to push away. Without the notion that "I" am dying, the experience is quite different. When each gasp is whole and complete in itself, because there is nothing to gain and nothing to lose, then death becomes no-death. Birth is not something that leads to death, and death is not something that birth has led to. We can realize this by "forgetting ourselves" in the way that Dogen described, to wake up as *just this* breath, *just that* gasp.

Realizing the "empty" nature of birthing and dying—which in this case means that there is no self that they happen *to*—means we do not juxtapose them, using each to devalue the other. Birthing and living are not poisoned because they lead to death. Dying is not poisoned because we regret the loss of life. Another way to express it is that there is living-and-dying in each moment, each thought, each feeling, each action.

This breaks down the stone wall between life and death. To dwell on the far side of that wall, with the indifferent shades of the dead, is to be paralyzed by awareness of death and one's futile craving for immortality. To knock the stones down and step over to the other side of that wall is to realize life and death are twins.

Who takes the lead in knocking down that wall? Not the king, nor the dragon, nor the wizards. It is Alder, who is nobody special. What becomes important about him, from a Buddhist perspective, is that he nonetheless has the same buddha-nature as the rest of them, and the rest of us. Zen, in particular, emphasizes that enlightenment does not make us special; on the contrary, we realize that we are like everyone else. Alder has even lost his modest healing powers, except one: he loves his departed wife so deeply. His love for Lily remains the most important thing in his life. He breaks down the wall to be with her, to die with her. But what's love got to do with it? Buddhism emphasizes compassion, not this kind of love.

If the true opposite of love is not hatred but fear, as we suggested near the end of Chapter 4, then to the extent that we are afraid we are also unable to love—yet perhaps that too can be turned around, in order to make love the means of our liberation from fear. Alder is not afraid of death, because all he cares about is being with Lily.

To love someone or something truly is another way to transcend fear, even fear of death, because when we love, our sense of self becomes devoted to the well-being of someone or something other than ourselves. Insofar as our love is genuine, the other's well-being becomes more important to us than our own well-being: more important than our fear of death, because more important than our death. Does Alder show us another path to liberation from ego?

Afterword

THE BUDDHA never taught Buddhism; he called what he taught the Dharma. The teachings that were later codified, ramifying into the traditions we now identify as Buddhist, do not exhaust that Dharma. Buddhism, as a spiritual teaching and path, is a form of the Dharma, but the truth of the Dharma remains greater than any of the symbol systems that attempt to convey it. How else does the Dharma express itself today?

The Telling, a recent science fiction novel by Ursula Le Guin, tells the story of Sully, an extraterrestrial anthropologist caught between two monolithic worlds. Terra, her home, has become a theocratic state governed by religious fundamentalists who bomb libraries. "Only one Word, only one Book. All other words, all other books were darkness, error. They were dirt. *Let the Lord shine out!* "[44]

Aka, her assigned world, has recently embraced a different kind of fundamentalism, outlawing all old customs and beliefs in order to pursue its dream of a materialistic and progressive society based on Pure Science. "It is the responsibility of every citizen, whether adult or student, to report reactionary teachings and to bring teachers who permit sedition or introduce irrationality and superstition in their classroom to the attention of the authorities" (8). Almost all books are confiscated and pulped as building material, and those who resist are sent to reeducation facilities. Even as Le Guin's Terra exaggerates the theocratic tendencies of some religious fundamentalists, Aka has obvious similarities with some communist regimes, but its rulers' preoccupation with technological progress has wider resonances. In place of the traditional "great consensual social pattern within which each individual sought physical and spiritual satisfaction, they had made it a great hierarchy in which each individual served the indefinite growth of the society's material wealth and prosperity. From an active homeostatic balance they had turned it to an active forward-thrusting imbalance" (119)—an imbalance familiar to consumers who never consume enough, to a society whose GNP is never big enough.

The governments of these two worlds may be opposites, but they share an intolerance of any other stories. The only story permitted is the monolithic one promulgated by the state. Yet Sully, after obtaining permission to venture into the outback, encounters some "criminal antiscientific cult societies" that teach her about what she comes to call the Telling.

She discovers that the traditional, premodern Akan worldview is a "religion-philosophy of the type of Buddhism or Taoism" that emphasizes process rather than rigidly distinguished things. This gives Le Guin an opportunity to spell out her own ideal religion:

On Aka, *God* is a word without referent. No capital letters. No creator, only creation. No eternal father to reward or punish, justify injus-

tice, ordain cruelty, offer salvation. Eternity not an endpoint but a con-
tinuity. Primary division of being into material and spiritual only as two-
as-one, or one in two aspects. No hierarchy of Nature and Supernatural.
No binary Dark/Light, Evil/Good, or Body/Soul. No afterlife, no rebirth,
no immortal disembodied or reincarnated soul. No heavens no hells. The
Akana system is a spiritual discipline with spiritual goals, but they're exactly the same goals it seeks for bodily and ethical well-being. Right action is its own end. Dharma without karma.... And good was an adjec-
tive, always: good food, good health, good sex, good weather. No capital letters. Good or Evil as entities, warring powers, never. (102, 105)

Not quite Buddhism, but pretty close. As a trained anthropologist, Sully continues to be struck by the differences from the other
religious systems she has studied. There are physical-mental exercises
like Yoga and Tai Chi, and trance states are sometimes cultivated,
yet people do not pray for anything. Their chants are better understood as litanies of praise for the beauty and richness of the natural
world. They do not sacrifice anything either, except money. Most
puzzling of all, she cannot discover the *doctrines* of this life-system.
"What was it these people believed? What was it they held sacred?
She kept looking for the core of the matter, the words at the heart
of the Telling, the holy books to study and memorize. She found
them, but not it. No Bible. No koran. Dozens of upanishads, a million sutras. Every maz [master] gave her something else to read....
There was no correct text. There was no standard version. Of anything (110–11)."

There is music and dance, painting and carving, yet most important of all (for Sully, at least, as for Le Guin) are the *words*. "The essential work of the maz, what gave them honor among the people, was telling: reading aloud, reciting, telling stories, and talking about the stories" (115).

Unlike the official religious and materialistic fundamentalisms enforced by the Terran and Akan authorities, there is no One Sacred Story (God, Science) that must be believed and venerated. Instead, an enormous number of stories, and types of stories, are told and respected, their teachings overlapping but not systematized. The point is not to cling to a story in order to be saved, but to retell that story, to keep it alive in the imagination of people who can live by it. If the stories are sacred, their Telling is no less sacred, and their hearing too.

Is the Telling another term for the Dharma? As Le Guin's explicit reference suggests, the many stories that compose Buddhism are an important part of the Telling, yet they do not exhaust it. We like to think that Le Guin's own tales are part of the great Telling, along with Tolkien's *The Lord of the Rings*, Ende's *Momo*, Miyazaki's *Nausicaa* and *Princess Mononoke*, and Pullman's *His Dark Materials*. None of these other fantasies refers to Buddhism by name, but we have tried to show that each brings some aspect of the Dharma to life in a way that speaks to contemporary people. Undoubtedly, other recent fantasies and stories could have been discussed, and we may confidently expect that more will be written (and filmed) in the future. If we are as openminded as the Buddha himself wanted us to be, we will be able to appreciate them and benefit from their different ways of bringing the Dharma to life.

Notes

1 "The famous episode of the Buddha's seeing, allegedly for the first time in his life, 'the four Sights'—a sick man, an old man, a corpse and a renouncer—and his subsequent departure from home as an ascetic... is not told at length of Gotama in any extant commentary before the commentarial period, although there is a short autobiographical text at A[nguttara Nikaya] I 145–6 which seems to presuppose the story." Steven Collins, *Nirvana and Other Buddhist Felicities* (Cambridge: Cambridge University Press, 1998), 351.

2 *The Letters of J. R. R. Tolkien*, ed. Humphrey Carpenter with Christopher Tolkien (Boston: Houghton Mifflin, 1981), 147.

3 Ibid., 76; cited in the text hereafter as L. Titles by Tolkien are abbreviated as *FR: Fellowship of the Ring* (London: George Allen and Unwin, 1954); *TT: The Two Towers* (London: George Allen and Unwin, 1954); *RK: Return of the King* (London: George Allen and Unwin, 1956).

4 J. R. R. Tolkien, *Tree and Leaf* (London: George Allen and Unwin, 1964), 5.

5 Randel Helms, *Tolkien's World* (London: Thames and Hudson, 1974), 8, 12.

6 Humphrey Carpenter, *J. R. R. Tolkien: A Biography* (London: George Allen and Unwin, 1977), 151.

7 Tolkien, quoted in Helms, *Tolkien's World,* 132.

8 Tolkien, *Tree and Leaf,* 57–62.

9   See Helms, *Tolkien's World*, especially Chapters 4 and 5, to which this section is indebted.

10 Ibid., 75.

11 Dhammapada, verses 1–2. *Dhammapada, The: The Sayings of the Buddha,* trans. and ed. Thomas Byrom (Boulder, Colorado: 1993).

12 In modern moral theory, for example, utilitarian theories focus on consequences, deontological theories focus on moral principles such as the Golden Rule, and "virtue theories" focus on one's character and motivations.

13 Joe Robinson, "Four Weeks Vacation," *Utne Reader,* September–October 2000.

14 Robert Levine, *A Geography of Time* (New York: Basic Books, 1997), 107.

15 Michael Ende, *The Neverending Story,* trans. Ralph Mannheim (London: Allen Lane, 1983).

16 Michael Ende, *Momo,* trans. J. Maxwell Brownjohn (London: Puffin, 1984), 55 (hereafter cited in the text).

17 Ende visited Japan several times, and became interested in Buddhism. His first visit in 1977 included a discussion with a Zen priest.

18 Nagarjuna, *Sunyatasaptati,* verse 58, personal translation.

19 Nagarjuna, *Mulamadhyamikakarika* 13:5, in Candrakirti, *Lucid Exposition of the Middle Way,* trans. Mervyn Sprung (Boulder, Colo.: Prajna, 1979).

20 Quoted in *The Soto Approach to Zen,* ed. Reiho Matsunaga (Tokyo: Layman Buddhist Society, 1958), 68.

21 Tanahashi, Kazuaki, ed., *Moon in a Dewdrop: Writings of Zen Master Dogen* (San Francisco: North Point, 198576–80; trans. altered).

22 E. E. Evans-Pritchard, *The Nuer* (New York: Oxford University Press, 1969), 103.

23 Anthony Aveni, *Empires of Time* (New York: Kodansha, 1995), 135.

24 Ibid., 331.

25 Ibid., 332.

26 Damian Thompson, *The End of Time* (London: Minerva), 325.

27 Quoted in Robert Levine, *A Geography of Time* (New York: Basic Books, 1997), 204–5.

28 Dhammapada, verses 3–5.

29 Helen McCarthy, *Hayao Miyazaki: Master of Japanese Animation* (Berkeley: Stone Bridge, 1999), 138.

30 Ibid., 74, 78.

31 Ibid., 193.

32 Miyazaki's comment, in Ibid., 203.

33 Ibid., 199.

34 We have been unable to trace the source of this quotation, which was included in an email.

35 *Momo*, 144.

36 Philip Pullman, *The Amber Spyglass* (New York: Ballantine, 2000), 28 (hereafter cited in the text).

37 Brahmajala Sutra I.i.17–19, Digha Nikaya, in Maurice Walshe, trans. and ed., *The Long Discourses of the Buddha: A Translation of the Digha Nikaya,* (Boston: Wisdom, 1995), pp. 75–76.

38 Thich Nhat Hanh, *The Heart of Understanding* (Berkeley, CA: Parallax Press, 1988), 3–5.

39 "Genjo koan," trans. Dan Welch and Kazuaki Tanahashi, in *Moon in a Dewdrop: Writings of Zen Master Dogen,* ed. Kazuaki Tanahashi (San Francisco: North Point, 1985), 70. For more on the interpretation of lack in Buddhism, see David Loy, *Lack and Transcendence: The Problem of Death and Life in Psychotherapy, Existentialism, and Buddhism* (Amherst, N.Y.: Humanity Books, 1996).

40 Ursula K. Le Guin, *The Wizard of Earthsea* (New York: Parnassus, 1968), 197–98, 199.

41 Ursula K. Le Guin, *The Other Wind* (New York: Harcourt, 2001), 153-54 (hereafter cited in the text).

42 Tanahashi, *Moon in a Dewdrop*, 93–94.

43 Ibid., 74.

44 Ibid., 75.

46 Ursula K. Le Guin, *The Telling* (New York: Harcourt, 2000), 4–5 (hereafter cited in the text).

Bibliography

Bassham, Gregory and Eric Bronson, eds. The *Lord of the Rings and Philosophy: One Book to Rule Them All* (Chicago, Illinois: Open Court, 2003).

Candrakirti, *Lucid Exposition of the Middle Way*, trans. Mervyn Sprung (Boulder, Colorado: Prajna, 1979).

Carpenter, Humphrey, *J. R. R. Tolkien: A Biography* (London: George Allen and Unwin, 1977).

Carpenter, Humphrey with Christopher Tolkien, eds. *The Letters of J. R. R. Tolkien* (Boston: Houghton Mifflin, 1981).

Collins, Steven, *Nirvana and Other Buddhist Felicities* (Cambridge: Cambridge University Press, 1998).

Dhammapada, The: The Sayings of the Buddha, trans. and ed. Thomas Byrom (Boulder, Colorado: 1993).

Ende, Michael, *Momo*, trans. J. Maxwell Brownjohn, (London: Penguin, 1986).

Ende, Michael, *The Neverending Story*, trans. Ralph Mannheim (London: Allen Lane, 1983).

Evans-Pritchard, E. E., *The Nuer* (New York: Oxford University Press, 1969).

Hanh, Thich Nhat, *The Heart of Understanding* (Berkeley: Parallax Press, 1988).

Helms, Randel, *Tolkien's World* (London: Thames and Hudson, 1974).

Le Guin, Ursula K., *The Farthest Shore* (New York: Victor Gollancz, 1973).

———, *The Other Wind* (New York: Harcourt, 2001).

———, *Tales of Earthsea* (New York: Harcourt, 2001).

———, *Tehanu* (New York: Atheneum, 1991).

———, *The Telling* (New York: Harcourt, 2000).

———, *The Tombs of Atuan* (New York: Victor Gollancz, 1972).

———, *The Wizard of Earthsea* (New York: Parnassus, 1968).

Levine, Robert, *A Geography of Time* (New York: Basic Books, 1997).

Loy David, *Lack and Transcendence: The Problem of Death and Life in Psychotherapy, Existentialism, and Buddhism* (Amherst, New York: Humanity Books, 1996).

Matsunaga, Reiho, ed. *The Soto Approach to Zen* (Tokyo: Layman Buddhist Society, 1958).

McCarthy, Helen, *Hayao Miyazaki: Master of Japanese Animation* (Berkeley: Stone Bridge, 1999).

Milton, John, ed. John Leonard, *Paradise Lost* (Harmondsworth: Penguin Classics, 2003).

Mori, Yoko, "Michael Ende Biography," trans. Miguel Yasuyuki Hirota (2001), at www.geocities.com/Athens/Academy/2432/uk.michael.html

Pullman, Philip, *The Amber Spyglass* (New York: Ballantine, 2000).

———, *The Golden Compass* (New York: Ballantine, 1995).

———, *The Subtle Knife* (New York: Ballantine, 1997).

Robinson, Joe, "Four Weeks Vacation," *Utne Reader,* September–October 2000.

Tanahashi, Kazuaki, ed., *Moon in a Dewdrop: Writings of Zen Master Dogen* (San Francisco: North Point, 1985).

Thompson, Damian, *The End of Time* (London: Minerva, 1996).

Tolkien, J. R. R., *Fellowship of the Ring* (London: George Allen and Unwin, 1954).

——, *Return of the King* (London: George Allen and Unwin, 1956).

——, *The Silmarillion* (New York: Del Rey, 1990).

——, *Tree and Leaf* (London: George Allen and Unwin, 1964).

——, *The Two Towers* (London: George Allen and Unwin, 1954).

Walshe, Maurice, trans. and ed., *The Long Discourses of the Buddha: A Translation of the Digha Nikaya* (Boston: Wisdom, 1995).

Nixon Under the Bodhi Tree and Other Works of Buddhist Fiction
Edited by Kate Wheeler
Foreword by
Charles Johnson
288 pages,
ISBN 0-86171-354-0,
$16.95

"★[starred review]. You'll relish the beauty of these well-told tales. Wheeler has assembled a stellar collection, one that fans of fiction and Buddhism hope for—full of play, insight, revelation, and diversity, and never compromising in delight."
—*Publishers Weekly*

Pico Iyer, Victor Pelevin, Doris Dorrie and other renowned contributors join young award-winners in what National Book Award-winner Charles Johnson calls "an embarrassment of literary riches," sure to please fiction lovers of every stripe. From the O. Henry Award-winning title story, to visionary short-shorts and barely fictionalized personal memoirs, *Nixon Under the Bodhi Tree and Other Works of Buddhist Fiction* is inventive, exciting, and unlike any collection before it.

"This volume is surely a milestone in Western Buddhist literature—and a book that fiction lovers, Buddhist or otherwise will very much enjoy."—*Tricycle: The Buddhist Review*

Novice to Master:
An Ongoing Lesson in the
Extent of My Own Stupidity
Soko Morinaga
Translated by
Belenda Attaway Yamakawa
144 pages,
ISBN 0-86171-393-1, $11.95

"I'm a real fan of *Novice to Master*. This wise and warm book should be read by all."—Anthony Swofford, author of *Jarhead*

"Sometimes a book comes along with a title that dares you *not* to pick it up. In the case of *Novice to Master*, it was the subtitle—*An Ongoing Lesson in the Extent of My Own Stupidity*. Morinaga's telling of his life from youth in Japan's army during World War II to becoming a Zen master is direct, blessedly free of jargon, and sprinkled with universal spiritual observations. There are passages that had me laughing out loud; others inspired serious reflection. Remarkable: pithy, profound, inspiring, and joyous."—*Arkansas Democrat Gazette*

"Part memoir, part wisdom resource, *Novice to Master* provides a lively and enlightening overview of Zen, and wonderful anecdotes on the poignance of living in the present moment." —*Spirituality and Health*

"One can't help but be drawn to the genuine tone of Morinaga's voice and his sense of humor."—*Shambhala Sun*

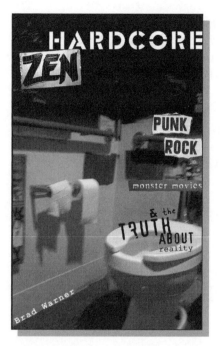

Hardcore Zen: Punk Rock, Monster Movies, and the Truth About Reality
Brad Warner
224 pages,
ISBN 0-86171-380-X, $14.95

"Man oh man, this is a VERY good book."—Janwillem van de Wetering, author of *The Empty Mirror* and *The Corpse on the Dike*

★"Warner, an early-'80s hardcore punk musician, discovered Zen in college, moved to Japan to make B-grade monster movies, and eventually became a bona fide Zen master by formally receiving 'dharma transmission.' Yet true to his punk spirit, he relentlessly demands that all teaching, all beliefs, all authority—including his own—must be questioned. His book is by turns wickedly funny, profane, challenging and iconoclastic—but always with genuine kindness. Entertaining, bold and refreshingly direct, this book is likely to change the way one experiences other books about Zen—and maybe even the way one experiences reality."—*Publishers Weekly* [starred review]

"*Hardcore Zen* is *Be Here Now* for now."—*Tricycle*

"For my money, *Hardcore Zen* is worth two or three of those Buddhism-for-Young-People books."—*Shambhala Sun*

Mindfulness in Plain English:
Revised, Expanded Edition
Bhante Gunaratana
224 pages,
ISBN 0-86171-321-4, $14.95

"Extremely up-to-date and approachable, this book also serves as a very thorough FAQ for new (and not-so-new) meditators. Bhante has an engaging delivery and a straight-forward voice that's hard not to like."—*Shambhala Sun*

"Of great value to newcomers, especially people without access to a teacher."—Larry Rosenberg, Director, Cambridge Insight Meditation Center

Zen Meditation in Plain English
John Daishin Buksbazen
Foreword by Peter Matthiessen
128 pages, ISBN 0-86171-316-8, $12.95

"Down-to-earth advice about the specifics of Zen meditation: how to position the body; how and when to breathe; what to think about. Includes helpful diagrams and even provides a checklist to help beginners remember all of the steps. A fine introduction, grounded in tradition yet adapted to contemporary life."
—*Publishers Weekly*

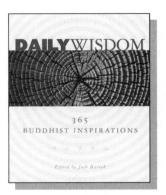

Daily Wisdom
365 Buddhist Inspirations
Edited by Josh Bartok
384 pages, ISBN 0-86171-300-1,
$16.95

Daily Wisdom draws on the richness of Buddhist writings to offer a spiritual cornucopia that will illuminate and inspire day after day, year after year. Sources span a spectrum from ancient sages to modern teachers, from monks to lay people, from East to West, from poetry to prose. Each page, and each new day, reveals another gem of *Daily Wisdom.*

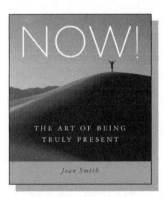

NOW!
The Art of Being Truly Present
Jean Smith
144 pages, ISBN 0-86171-480-6,
$14.00

These "mindful reminders" from Jean Smith—who has introduced so many to the benefits of mindfulness and meditation—help us to be truly present in every wonderful moment. A great gift!

"Eighty-four aspirational passages for applying Buddhist teachings directly to what ails you, as well as nurturing positive qualities."—*Tricycle*

The Great Awakening
A Buddhist Social Theory
David R. Loy
240 pages,
ISBN 0-86171-366-4, $16.95

"Now that I'm growing old, I look for deeper meaning everywhere. Loy's book sure gave me some—not only on that personal, how-to-live-my-life level, but also in the universal realm of what's-this-all-about."—Kalle Lasn, Editor-in-Chief of *Adbusters* Magazine and author of *Culture Jam: The Uncooling of America*

"There have been many attempts to understand modern social theory from a Buddhist perspective, but they have not been satisfactory because they were either written by scholars well versed in Buddhist teachings but not with the outside world, or vice versa. Loy, however, seems to bring together an deep understanding of both. More importantly, he displays a sympathetic attitude to both Theravada and Mahayana (as well as Taoist) teachings which gives this book a transcendental relevance. Loy argues that while Buddhism lacks an intrinsic social theory, its teachings do have important economic (and therefore political and social) implications that can help us respond to the New World Order."—*Eastern Horizon*

"With fruitful results, Loy shows that Buddhist social theory is neither wishful thinking nor a mechanical exercise in trying to match past teachings to present problems...*The Great Awakening* is arguably the most extensive response to 9/11 published to date. Timely...a formidable critique of Western social thought."—*Tricycle*

Wisdom Publications

Wisdom Publications, a nonprofit publisher, is dedicated to preserving and transmitting important works from all the major Buddhist traditions as well as works on related East-West themes.

To learn more about Wisdom, or browse our books on-line, visit our website at wisdompubs.org. You may request a copy of our mail-order catalog on-line or by writing to:

Wisdom Publications
199 Elm Street
Somerville, Massachusetts 02144 USA
Telephone: (617) 776-7416
Fax: (617) 776-7841
Email: info@wisdompubs.org
www.wisdompubs.org

Wisdom is a nonprofit, charitable 501(c)(3) organization affiliated with the Foundation for the Preservation of the Mahayana Tradition (FPMT).